Orange Street & Brickhole Lane

ORANGE STREET
&
BRICKHOLE LANE

Ralph Arnold

RUPERT HART-DAVIS
SOHO SQUARE LONDON
1963

Printed in Great Britain by
The Camelot Press Ltd., London and Southampton

Chapter One

I HAD been told about the invasion of the village by a party of forty children from one of the County Primary Schools in Rochester, six miles away. Aged between eight and ten, they had arrived in the morning, had split up into small groups, and had spent the day examining the church, the college, and other buildings of interest, going round one of the farms, being shown the processes of hop-picking and hop-drying, observing bird and animal life, collecting botanical, geological, and entomological specimens, sketching, and asking the villagers questions. People had been impressed by their orderly behaviour, by their industry, by their enthusiasm, and by their excellent manners. They were engaged, they had explained, on a village survey.

A week or so later their form-master rang me up. I had been in London when the children had visited Cobham and, as I had once written a book about the village, my absence had apparently been a matter of regret to the surveyors. They had hoped to "interview" me. Would it be possible, I was asked, for a small contingent to come over specially to see me?

I viewed this event with some alarm. I found it difficult to believe that the kind of history with which my book had dealt could possibly interest small children who, as I understood it, lived in a new building estate on the outskirts of a large town. I simply could not imagine what I should find to say to them.

The day came, and three little boys and three little girls were shepherded into my room. We were solemnly introduced; and most of the children sat on a sofa. Their feet did not reach the floor, and they looked rather like a row of swallows perching on a telegraph line. Each child clutched a pencil and a notebook. Two of them, flatteringly, had battered library copies of my own book. All of them regarded me with steady, unwinking stares.

Distinctly unnerved by this unusual audience, I haltingly began to tell them what the village of Cobham in Kent may have looked like, and may have been like, one hundred, two hundred, and three hundred years ago; and what kind of a life the villagers must have led when there had been no buses, no trains, and deplorably bad roads. I tried to explain what the farms had been like at different times, and how they had been worked. I told them, as best I could, the stories of the church, of Cobham Hall, and of the chantry college of St Mary's which, after the Reformation, had turned into the almshouses which they had visited. Tentatively—because I know next to nothing about prehistory—I told them something about the supposed megalith in Battle Street; and I mentioned the remains of the Roman villa in Cobham Park, and the paved Roman road that runs along the north boundary of the parish. I explained, though I cannot imagine why I thought it would interest them, that in the course of years there had been three different schools in the village, and four different vicarages. And I showed them an account book kept by a yeoman farmer in the parish covering the years between 1736 and 1741. I pointed out that his excellently clear handwriting was very like George Bernard Shaw's.

I was astonished when they told me—I had expected a dead silence when I stopped talking—that they had been lent a similar account book which had belonged to the village miller in the 1830s, a document which, had I known of its existence, would have been of great interest and value to me when I was writing my book. They promised me a sight of it. They informed me that the Ship Inn at the top of the village street had been called the Ship Inn because the cottages it had replaced had been built from ships' timbers. I had never discovered that

6

for myself. And they asked me if I had ever tried to crawl along the secret passage that leads from the college to the cellars of the Darnley Arms public house. I felt bound to tell them that I thought that this tunnel had probably served as a drain, and not as an escape route; and that I had never crawled along it.

Each child had prepared a list of specific questions. Most of these questions were sensible and to the point; a few of them I was even able to answer. But one or two were splendidly and wildly irrelevant. Were there, I was asked, any marble buildings in the village? And, much more surprisingly, did I keep a housemaid? This odd inquiry came from one of the small girls. I have never been able to decide what prompted it.

The business of the day over, the children took a deep and flattering interest in the contents and furnishings of my room, in my Basenji dog, and in myself. They wanted to know how many books I owned. And how many rooms there were in my house. I failed to give a satisfactory answer to either of these questions. I was allowed to get away with a suggestion that I had, perhaps, a thousand books; but I was made to go through the house, room by room, and the result was carefully noted. How many books had I written? All too many, I said; but again I was not allowed to escape so easily, and a careful count had to be conducted. How much money had I made out of them? I satisfied them, more or less, by telling them that when I was very young I wrote three boys' adventure stories, the copyright of which I sold to Messrs. Blackie for £50 a time. I am uncertain whether they considered this too much or too little. "Mr Arnold," their form-master told them, "is a publisher. He works in London, and only comes down to Cobham at week-ends." They wanted to know how long I had been a publisher, and what I did. Did I print books? I said that I had been in publishing for twenty-five years; and that I was going to retire quite soon. I explained that I did not print books. I helped to decide what books my firm would publish, someone else printed them, and then we did our best to sell them. This did not sound a very convincing explanation of a somewhat complicated calling. When the time came for the children to go away, my wife and I were formally invited to come and see the "Village Exhibition" which they were going to stage at their school.

This exhibition, ranged round the walls of two adjoining class-rooms in a brand new school building that was all glass, chromium and bright paint, was an eye-opener. It was aston- ishingly comprehensive and extremely well arranged. Each group of surveyors had been responsible for its own specialized section. Each individual exhibit was neatly and clearly labelled, with well-written and well-expressed explanatory notes. What I liked especially about these explanatory notes was that they said straight out exactly what they set out to say—with no evasions or beatings about the bush.

We were taken round by our six visitors, who assumed the proprietorial airs of hosts and hostesses, the small boys expertly manœuvring my wheelchair up any steps that we encountered. The thirty-four other surveyors hovered in the background. Rightly, I was allowed to miss nothing—from exhibit number one, a wall display of pressed leaves with the disarming caption: "These are some of the specimens we found. Some others were thrown away by mistake"; to the life story, in photographs, of one of the village boys who was training to be a mounted policeman.

It was an exhibition designed to show what the village is like today, and what it had been like at different times in the past. I was greatly impressed by how sensible and practical their approach had been. As far as the past was concerned, they (or, as I suspected, their enterprising and intelligent form-master) had reached a fundamental conclusion. Prominently displayed was a large drawing of a triangle, with sides of equal length. Along the base was printed the word CHURCH: along one side was printed the word VILLAGE: and the third side was labelled HALL. Underneath the triangle, to rub the point in, was the drawing of a three-legged stool, with each leg similarly captioned. "In

8

olden days," the explanation ran, "Cobham was like a triangle or a three-legged stool. If any one of the legs or sides had been missing, the rest would not have worked properly."

The present was dominated by the children's curious passion for statistics—evidence of which I had already experienced. They had discovered exactly how long all the people they had interviewed had lived in Cobham, how old they were, and how many children they had—living and dead. They had also asked them, evidently, whether they were happy in their lives and in their work. These questions had produced some forthright answers. One villager had told them that he had "lived in Cobham for thirty years and didn't like it"; and a farm worker had explained that his calling was "tricky but not hard". They had set down the exact number of the livestock on the farm they had been shown round; and they had conducted a traffic census in Cobham Street, illustrated by a graph. From the church register they had discovered that in the year 1759 there had been sixteen baptisms and fifteen burials. In 1959 the corresponding figures had been twenty-four and eight—"So we think that Cobham's population is growing, but we cannot be sure, because we should have found the figures for more years if we had had the time." They had also copied out all the names that appear on monuments inside the church, noting the names that occurred most often. Three thrushes had been observed, twenty-four sparrows, one starling, thirty swifts, and two pigeons.

They had traced the stories of the church, the college, the Hall, the windmill, all the public houses, the village pump, and the police sergeant. With the exception of the Hall—which, at the time, had been deemed unsafe and had been barred to them —they had personally inspected and explored all these landmarks. When we reached the section labelled "Hops" it was plain that they knew quite a lot about the processes of hop-growing, hop-picking and hop-drying; and the hop-drying expert, a mechanically-minded boy, was propelled to the front to explain a professional-looking diagram of the oast-house furnaces. The hop-dryer on duty on the occasion of their visit had apparently had his attention drawn to a passage in my book in which I quoted this extract from the diary of Richard Hayes, a Cobham yeoman farmer:

> *27 September 1761:* My hop-dryer has his victuals and drinks no small beer. One quart of mild at every meal and at night. Takes a quart bottle of beer out with him every night and is allowed a quart bottle of brandy to refresh himself during drying.

Mr Pye's hop-dryer had pertinently observed that he wished he had lived two hundred years earlier.

The form-master had made rubbings of the celebrated brasses in the chancel of the church; and the children had made drawings of its windows and of its other architectural features. Outstanding among a mass of pictures was a large painting of the outside of the church. I asked if the nine-year-old artist had copied it from a postcard. Not at all. He had made a detailed sketch on the ground, and had then worked it up at home. It was bold in execution and colour, very well composed, and remarkably effective.

To my embarrassment I found a section devoted to myself. There was a portrait, drawn from memory, which I tried hard to think of as a failure; and an accompanying "profile". "Mr Arnold himself," it began, "is a polite, well-spoken person, who is a publisher, and who writes books as well. Mr Arnold wears glasses and smokes a pipe. You can tell he is an author because he always describes a noun with an adjective when he speaks." An alarmingly perceptive observation from which, ever since I read it, I have tried unsuccessfully to profit.

Driving home from this "exhibition", I found myself regretting that no form-master at the preparatory school to which I myself had been sent at the age of eight and a half had had the wits and imagination to think up a similar project. Making a survey of Crowborough, and delving into the past of that prosperous parish, would have made a nice change from the dull walks which were the only alternatives to playing cricket, football, or hockey. I can recall no encouragement, while I was at the Beacon School, to take any interest in local affairs—though all on my own I developed a passion for the now-defunct Beacon Hotel, and was genuinely pained by the rejection out of hand of a perfectly serious suggestion that my parents should sell all that they had and take up permanent residence in it. I thought that the pleasures of the holidays would be greatly enhanced by eating meals in a dining-room full of little tables each of which had a pink silk-shaded electric lamp; and I was convinced that it would be splendid to spend the evenings in its lounge, which had palms in brass pots and smelt richly of cigar-smoke.

Nor were we encouraged to take an interest in natural history. Our excursions in this field, as far as I can remember, were confined to the rare occasions when someone had hit a six into the patch of gorse and bushes that adjoined the cricket ground. Then, while pretending to look for the missing cricket ball, we in fact searched diligently and enthusiastically for puss-moth caterpillars. When we found one of these furry, improbable-looking little dragons we shut it up in a leaf-filled container. The prisoners seldom survived for more than a few days. To my regret I have never succeeded in becoming anything of a naturalist.

After I had got home that evening, and while the "exhibition" was still very much in my mind, another thought struck me. I remembered the "profile", and I began to think about the impression that I must have made on the six children who had come out to Cobham to see me. None of them, I imagined, had ever encountered either a writer or a publisher before; and for better or worse I must have given them some kind of an image of myself. As likely as not they had gone away with a picture in their mind's eye of someone who, when he was in London, picked books as one might pick gooseberries, had them printed, and then sold them in the same way as cigarettes or chocolates are sold in a shop. They probably thought that when I was at home at week-ends I spent all my time either surveying the village of Cobham, or sitting at my desk writing books. They might well have gained an impression, if they had thought about it at all, that this was money for jam, and not half a bad kind of life. One or two of them might even have entertained a vague idea that when they grew up they would quite like to be a writer, or a publisher, or an amateur historian or, like myself, a hybrid mixture of all three. And it there and then occurred to me that when I retired from publishing I might do worse than try to give some account of how I had stumbled into the three major interests and enthusiasms of my life—writing, publishing, and historical research.

Chapter Two

IN the summer of 1945, at the Headquarters of South East
Asia Command, at Kandy, in Ceylon, when we had endlessly discussed what each of us would do when the war had
ended and we had returned home, I had always said that under
no circumstances would I go back to publishing. On the face
of it, and in the light of the difficulties that I had encountered in
gaining a foothold in the publishing profession, this was a
strange decision to have reached.

It is common knowledge that, to a certain type of young
man, publishing acts as an irresistible magnet. I was a perfect
example of that type of young man. From as far back as I can
remember I had had a passion for books. As a very small boy I
used to insist on having all the Beatrix Potter stories, and L.
Leslie Brooke's *Johnny Crow's Garden*, read aloud to me so often
that I knew them by heart. After I had learnt to read for myself,
I devoured everything and anything that I could lay my hands
on—all E. Nesbit's books, stories like Mrs Ewing's *Jackanapes*,
that had belonged to my mother, bound volumes of *Punch*, and
the Army and Navy Co-operative Stores Catalogue. Reading
soon became more than a mere pleasurable pastime. I found that
it was a very present help in trouble. My preparatory school
taught me that. In the terrible interval between the end of luncheon on the last day of the holidays and the car coming round
to take me back to Crowborough, I could only be consoled,
more or less, by one of the *Irish R.M.* stories—"The Man who
came to buy Apples" was my favourite. And it was also at
Crowborough that I first discovered the therapeutic virtues of

the detective story. I was nine years old, and I had made a terrible mistake. A week after returning for my third term I had written to tell my mother that I hated school and was miserably unhappy there. It had been rather a good letter for, although my handwriting was execrable, I already had the pen of an all-too ready writer. Once I had got this letter off my chest I immediately cheered up and began once more to enjoy myself very much indeed. I had a great many friends, and to my immense pride I was elected to membership of the Motor-car Club. This was by way of a stiff examination. Pictures of various motor-cars, minus their captions, were cut out of *The Motor* and *The Autocar*, and the candidate had to identify the make of each of them. So it had been an unpleasant shock to get a letter from my mother that morning saying that she was not surprised that I was unhappy, because she had always thought it was rather a dull and unenterprising school; that she had rushed round and had found a more congenial establishment that would take me in at once; and that she was driving over after luncheon that very day to have it out with the headmaster and to take me away. The prospect of being removed from the jungle I knew, and of being precipitated into a new, strange jungle—and in mid-term at that —was intolerable and not to be borne. And I realized that in refusing to budge, a course on which I was determined, I would run into very bad trouble indeed—trouble with my mother, and trouble of a much more serious nature with the headmaster.

Alone in an empty, echoing form-room, awaiting the inevitable summons to the headmaster's drawing-room—everyone else was playing cricket—I read Conan Doyle's *The Speckled Band*. Detective fiction, ever since, has consoled me in such trials as very occasional bouts of sleeplessness, and those ghastly first nights spent in nursing homes and hospitals.

I also developed a precocious taste for writing. Rather later on in my career at Crowborough I wrote a detective story myself. It was strong on character but a bit weak on plot. The heroine was the mother of a Roumanian school-fellow. This elegant lady had, unlike my own parents, taken up permanent residence at the Beacon Hotel. Swathed in sables, wearing Russian fur-lined boots, and smelling strongly of Parma violets, she used to pace the touchline of an afternoon, watching us playing association football. She captivated me entirely; and it was heartless of me to kill her off in her hotel bedroom. A blood-stained pink silk lampshade was the principal clue; but I cannot now recall who committed the crime, or why. At my public school, when I had got into the sixth form, I wrote a good deal of verse which was published in the pages of *The Lorettonian*, after I had taken the precaution of becoming its editor. It was either verse of a descriptive nature—trees figured in it a lot—or else serious stuff with a distinctly morbid tendency. "The Church Tower" had a foot in both camps:

> And once through the square wooden door
>   He thrillingly saw
> That he'd beaten the avenue trees,
>   For all these were below,
> He above. Did man know
>   The sensation of flying, the pace,
> The rushing through murmuring space,
>   The leaves' soft embrace?

Man—or the man about whom this poem was written—very soon found out, for he committed suicide by throwing himself off the leads. Even my "landscape" verses were pretty gloomy, and I cannot imagine why. I was not a morbid boy.

At Oxford I wrote one, and only one, short story which was accepted by a short-lived literary magazine published by Basil Blackwell. It was rather sad, too; which again was odd because it reflected a cheerful and extremely enjoyable affair of the heart which was occupying my mind at the time. It ended with the death of its hero while climbing down, *via* a magnolia, from his young lady's bedroom.

After leaving Oxford I went to learn German at an informal

kind of home-from-home establishment at Kitzbühel, in the Austrian Tirol. Tennerhof, a châlet on the lower slopes of Kitzbühler Horn, was, as it turned out, a hive of literary endeavour. Our host and tutor was Ernan Forbes Dennis, a good-looking, musical, artistic and altogether delightful man, who had married Phyllis Bottome, the Anglo-American novelist. Phyllis was the first professional writer I had ever encountered; and for me she has always remained the quintessence of what a professional writer should be. When I think of professional writers I think of her. To her husband's pupils—and we must have been very bad observers, for her successive volumes of autobiography have shown how wrong we were—she seemed to have had little or no contact with real life as we then understood that term. Owing to persistent and doggedly fought ill-health, she generally stayed in bed until lunchtime, writing rapidly. During the afternoon what she had written in longhand was typed out by her Austrian secretary. Sometimes, in the evenings, she would take me for a short walk, in the course of which she would weave remarkable fantasies round the owners of the various castles which we saw in the distance. A passing glimpse of these Austrian aristocrats, or the hint of some exciting irregularity in their private lives, enabled her, in her imagination, to conjure up a whole ready-made, well-rounded story of passion and adventure. That, I still think, is what being a novelist means. She was deeply interested in people; and she had, and still has, the gift of being compellingly readable.

Ian Fleming was one of my fellow students at the Tennerhof. His bedroom was awash with letters, opened and unopened, that he had received from admiring ladies of all ages; and at this stage of his career he was a devotee of *avant-garde* literature. Enviable first editions that he collected lay about on chairs and tables, together with copies of advanced literary journals like *Blast*. He learnt German much quicker and spoke it much better than I did, he skied much better, played tennis much better, and had a much greater success with the girls. He was extremely amusing, a very good friend, and I was devoted to him. Also living in the house, and doing lessons with a young German tutor whose face was covered with duelling scars, was Nigel Dennis, Ernan's nephew. I have often wondered since what, as a boy, he made of us. Though in reality shy and desperately uncertain of ourselves, we probably gave an appearance of being arrogant, worldly-wise, tiresome, and distressingly bumptious.

Austria went completely to my head. In the summer we used to go down to the Café Reisch every Thursday evening and sit drinking sherry cobblers while the natives of the small and still unspoilt town marched cheerfully and noisily up and down the main street behind their brass band. In the winter there were week-end expeditions when we struggled up the Hahnenkamm with the help of skins attached to our skis. We generally spent a couple of nights in alpine huts, and then got down again as best we could on Sunday afternoon. We were always careful to include an elderly guide in our party. He carried most of the provisions. And, if possible, we asked the very nice district nurse to join us—in case someone broke a leg. We got to know all the curious people who, for one reason or another, had come to live in Kitzbühel. There was a young man who lodged over the *Buchbinderei* and who, appropriately, was engaged in writing a novel. There were also several deposed royalties. Something that one of them once said in the middle of a tea-party has stuck in my mind. "My brother-in-law, the ex-King of Würtemburg," he told me, "has a piano as big as this room, and *it sounds like bells.*"

In the spring, when the thaw set in, I took a fortnight off and went down to Merano, in the Alto Adige. It was snowing at the top of the Brenner Pass. Going down the other side was like rushing through the months of March, April and May in the space of a few hours. The valley between Bolzano and Merano was a sea of peach blossom. From Merano I paid my first visit to Venice. This should have been a rather emancipated and dashing enterprise, for I had persuaded two Austrian sisters to come with me; but at the last moment we were joined by a couple of effective chaperons in the shape of the English resident chaplain and his wife. We all stayed in a very curious pension.

At the opening of the tennis season there was a grand tournament held on the hard courts under the frowning battlements of Schloss Kapps. Ian Fleming had maliciously and untruthfully spread it abroad that I was the British Southern Counties lawn tennis champion. My opening single against Graf Schlick, a very useful local player, was watched by a large audience, who must have been sadly disappointed. Early one morning in May we drove to Salzburg. It was one of those days of enchantment that are encountered once or twice in a lifetime. I have no doubt that the mountain scenery we drove through was extremely beautiful; but the limestone gorges with green water pouring over light grey rocks, the grey-green willows, the shining peaks and crags above the ranked masses of dark fir trees, and the villages with their elaborate inn signs and with flowers in pots on all the balconies, seemed to me to belong to another world. We ate our picnic lunch on the edge of a hayfield above a blue lake. There were sheets of gentians; and in the field itself there seemed to be more wild flowers than grass. Cow-bells tinkled, and down in the valley there were little onion-spired churches. I watched a ribbon of white road, expecting at any moment to see the Rolls-Royce touring car that would be conveying Dornford Yates's Richard Chandos on one of his romantic forays.

I wrote one short story while I was at Tennerhof. It was a satirical story about a party of ill-assorted English tourists, including a sanctimonious canon, who had embarked on the Hahnenkahnbahn and who were tricked into thinking that something had gone wrong with the machinery, and that in a few minutes their cable-car would fall, and they would be dashed to their deaths. Rather surprisingly *The Bystander* bought it, and paid me twenty-five guineas. I bought a carpet for the morning-room at home with the proceeds, and the die was cast. I would be a writer.

But not, I decided, a whole time, professional writer, or at least not yet; for there was the looming hurdle of the Foreign Office exam which I was hoping, with decreasing confidence, to pass. And before I could sit for it I had to go to France in order to brush up my very shaky French. I stayed with a French family who owned a château in the middle of an extensive oak forest mid-way between Laval and Vitré. I got out of the train at Laval station on a blisteringly hot afternoon in July. Waiting to meet me was a Paris taxicab, driven by a typical Parisian taxi-driver. It was later explained to me that he was the cook's lover; and that when the family moved down to the country from their Paris appartement, the cook refused to come unless her taxi-driver came too. His Citroën cab proved immensely useful. Turning off the long straight road that ran through the forest we drove down an avenue of peeling plane trees, under an arch, and into the forecourt of a little spiky château built of pink granite. The family, and their other guests, were having tea under the huge oak tree that grew in the middle of this forecourt. There was Madame la Comtesse, a war-widow, who owned the château; there were her two sons, Monsieur le Comte and Monsieur le Vicomte—both a bit younger than myself; there were Monsieur Lucien and Mademoiselle Lulu, the bachelor great-uncle and spinster great-aunt who always spent their summers at Moncroi; there was a Swedish girl who was also supposed to be learning French; and there was the wife of an English diplomat and her very pretty daughter. After I had been introduced all round and had been given a cup of tea, a violent argument started, in which I could hardly have been expected to take a useful part, as to whether a girl who was expected next day was, or was not, a virgin.

Madame la Comtesse was exceedingly beautiful, and a saint. In Paris, where the family lived for most of the year, she devoted herself to good works among the very poor. At Moncroi, of a morning, she would wrap herself in one of her elaborate peignoirs and descend to the kitchen, a long black pigtail hanging down her back, to interview the cook about luncheon. After that she strolled round the garden. At half-past twelve she would descend once more, her black hair now bound round her head, and wearing a very smart summer dress. In the evening, when it got a bit cooler, she would often set out, teetering on the highest of high heels, to visit one of the "petits fermiers" on her estate. It was all very feudal. Half the livestock and half the crops belonged to the tenants, half to the landlord. At all hours small children straggled down the avenue leading to the château carrying ducks, hens, and sacks of provender. Living in the country was regarded by the family as a kind of stylized joke. There was no bath in the house, no running water, and only one excessively primitive lavatory. Every day Monsieur Lucien, very old and stiff and correct, with a white waxed moustache, a threadbare grey suit with the rosette of the Legion of Honour in its button-hole, and an immensely high stiff collar, and Mademoiselle Lulu, very small and with a face exactly like an incredibly ancient, withered and heavily rouged apple, would set out for a walk in the park. Mademoiselle Lulu always wore a high-necked blouse fortified by whalebone supports. They walked very slowly, with Monsieur Lucien carrying a camp stool. They took it in turns to sit on the stool, pretending to admire the view but really in order to rest their tottery legs. Meals took an interminable time—especially luncheon on Tuesdays when Monsieur le Curé, fat and red and distinctly of the people, was always invited to the château. The windows at the back of the house looked out on to the park, which ran down to join the forest in the most natural way in the world. The forest looked something like a sea, very green and humpy and swelling in the foreground, and getting bluer and bluer in the distance until it finally became confounded with the clouds and sky. At one side of the château was the *potager*, immensely neat, immensely productive, and with a bed of the biggest, stiffest and most magnificent zinnias I have ever seen. Each day seemed to be finer and hotter than the last.

Every morning, when I should have been studying French grammar, I sat at a wobbly table in the window of my bedroom, writing my first novel. This was an enlarged version of the short story I had written at Oxford. I can never see violet-coloured ink, or smell the smoke of a *Caporal* cigarette, without being reminded of *House with the Magnolias*. In the afternoons we either went down to the *étang* to bathe, or set off to drive immense distances to play tennis with the far-flung neighbours. The *étang*, reached by way of little dusty lanes so narrow that their hedges brushed the sides of the taxi, was a large pond at the edge of a grass field. There was always a fuss in case any of the bathers should be overcome by a *congestion*. This stemmed from the experience of a young American who had been staying at the château the year before. Entering the water too soon after a heavy meal he had—or so the story went—lost consciousness, and had been pulled out more dead than alive.

Moncroi also had its sporting traditions. Larks were shot with the assistance of a complicated arrangement of mirrors—"all done by mirrors" had, in this instance, a strictly practical application; and there was the classic story of the great wild boar hunt. A pack of *chiens de chasse*, headed, as I was assured, by a genuine English foxhound, had been assembled in the park and, when the home coverts had been drawn blank for *sangliers*, the enterprise had developed into a deer hunt. After the sole *chevreuil* had slipped quietly and unobserved away, it had been decided to have a shot at digging out a badger. The foxhound, at this point, the so much admired "Jackie", had disgraced itself by refusing to go to ground, sitting disapprovingly aloof while the field, to while away the time, had settled down to a game of bridge.

Tennis parties at the neighbouring châteaux were rather peculiar. You never knew from château to château what to expect. Sometimes there would be two or three impeccable hard courts, surrounded by professional wire-netting. Sometimes the sole and only court would have been sketchily marked out on the gravel in front of the house, with a front door pillar acting as one support for the net and a conveniently placed tree as the other. The standard of play was equally uneven. No one ever seemed to think it odd that we arrived packed tightly into the Paris taxi-cab. In between sets we drank glasses of white *porto*.

I enjoyed being at the Château de Moncroi very much indeed; but my failure to learn French properly put paid to all serious ideas of the Foreign Office as a career, and I joined the staff of the Royal Institute of International Affairs. It was while I was working at Chatham House that Heinemann's accepted my first novel for publication. And it was my acceptance-tea with Charles Sedley Evans, at 99 Great Russell Street, that made me perfectly certain that what I really wanted to be was a publisher.

Charlie Evans, I am convinced, was the best—far and away the best—publisher that I, personally, have ever known. He had been given the manuscript of my novel by a mutual friend (I then knew no publishers myself); and one day at luncheon at the Garrick Club this friend told me, casually, that Charlie had said that he quite liked it, and would be glad if I would ring him up. I rushed back to the office to put through one of the most momentous calls of my life. I remember that my hand shook so much that I could hardly hold the receiver. Evans suggested that I should come round to tea with him that afternoon. I reached 99 Great Russell Street far too early. Sitting on the edge of my chair in the dark but impressive Heinemann waiting-room, in a state of ill-suppressed euphoria, I pictured myself joining the select group of distinguished writers who then clustered round the base of the Heinemann windmill— I would be sharing that sacred ground with John Galsworthy, Somerset Maugham and J. B. Priestley. Ushered upstairs and into an enormous room I was quickly brought back to my senses. Evans was a small man, with a bald head like a speckled brown egg. He crackled with vitality. He had read *House with the Magnolias*, and knew all about it. It was full of faults, he told me; and by rights I ought to start at page one and write the whole thing over again. But he fancied that he divined a gleam of promise and, if I so wished, he would bring it out. He did not anticipate that it would set the Thames on fire. To have my novel published—and by Heinemann's of all publishers—was what at that moment I wanted more than anything else in the world.

Our business concluded, Charlie Evans proceeded to complete his conquest of an impressionable young man. He explained, over tea and toasted teacakes, that he spent the whole of every Saturday in bed, reading manuscripts. On Sundays he played golf. He had just come back from the South of France, where he had been staying with Somerset Maugham. He told me that Maugham, when he wrote a book, dashed off a first draft at a hand gallop. If, at this stage, he encountered any snags he simply left blank spaces on the page. When this first draft was finished, he put it away in a drawer of his desk and left it there for at least a month. At the end of that time he took it out, read it through once and once only, and then burnt this first effort before sitting down to write draft two. In draft two he conscientiously tackled all the difficulties that he had by-passed in draft one. Draft two, when it was finished, got the same treatment—incarceration, incubation, one quick reading, and then incineration. Draft three was the finished, final product. I have often wished that I possessed the courage and the patience to follow this admirable practice. Nowadays, I generally re-write my books two or three times, but I lack the guts to destroy the earlier drafts.

Smoking an after-tea cigarette, I gazed with awe and reverence at Evans's desk. It was littered with manuscripts; and one of them, in a pink folder, was mine. He asked me if I was writing a second novel. I told him, mendaciously, that I was. It would

23

have to be, he said, a good deal better than my first. He admitted proudly that he himself had once written a book. One book, and one only. When he said goodbye, he gave me a copy of William Bolitho's *Twelve Against the Gods*. I have it still. I went down the stairs at 99 Great Russell Street determined that, come what might, I would be a publisher. Publishing, I decided, as I walked back to St. James's Square, was the solution to all my problems. I would have a steady job and a steady income, thus resolving my parents' doubts and fears, and my own terror lest, if I became a wholetime writer, I should be unable to think of anything to write about. As a publisher, most of my working life would, presumably, be spent in reading—and reading was what I enjoyed more than anything else except writing. I could go on writing in my spare time. And I had a vision of myself, older, wiser and by now famous, entertaining authors to luncheon in the Savoy Grill, and giving them, *à la* C. S. Evans, a great deal of valuable advice.

My terror of being unable to think of anything to write about was very real. Writing, I then believed, depended on inspiration. An idea for a story or a novel dawned; and the rest was as easy as pie. But sometimes ideas refused to come. After I had finished my first novel, in my early days at Chatham House, I had gone back to Kitzbühel for a summer holiday. I had been convinced that, sitting outside the Café Reisch, I would find inspiration for novel number two. It had been a disastrous venture. The Forbes Dennises had left, and Tennerhof had been turned into a pension. It is nearly always a mistake to go back to a place where you have been especially happy. I had sat day after day, nibbling the end of my pencil, smoking Egyptian cigarettes, and drinking endless cups of coffee. The harder I had tried to think of an idea for a plot the blanker my mind had grown. I had developed an almost incessant headache and a chronic sore throat. Temporarily, at least, these two disappointing weeks had killed all my ambitions to become a professional writer.

Becoming a publisher, I discovered, was also a good deal

24

easier said than done; and it took me a very long time. I knew of no strings to pull; and I had no illusions about my lack of essential qualifications. I could see no particular reason why any publishing house should require my services, a point of view which a good many of them shared. At long last—and after I had succeeded in writing not only a second novel that was worse rather than better than the first, and the three boys' adventure stories that I sold outright to Blackie's—I was put in touch with a firm of chartered accountants who appeared to know of several publishers who might be in need of an untrained editorial assistant. Through these accountants' good offices, some rather odd interviews were arranged. I recall one elderly publisher who, to my surprise, wore a dashingly checked riding coat and tight cavalry twill trousers. If there had happened to be a horse standing about in Henrietta Street at the time, he could have sprung on to it at a moment's notice. In one or two instances the suggestion was made that I should invest quite a lot of money in my prospective employer's business. My mother's trustees—fortunately I had no capital of my own—recoiled in horror from several balance sheets which they examined. At long last, and completely out of the blue, I received a short, stiff note from Mr Otto Kyllmann, chairman of Constable's. If I would care to call upon him, he wrote, he would be prepared, without prejudice, to see me. The evident lack of enthusiasm in this method of approach intrigued me.

I had always taken a special interest in Constable's because their business premises, in Orange Street, lay on my regular route from Chatham House to the Garrick Club. Day after day, as I walked to lunch, I would stop outside Number 10 to examine the new books displayed in the Constable window. I followed the fortunes of their publications—as indeed I followed the fortunes of all new books—in the review and advertisement columns of the Sunday newspapers and the weeklies. There was little at this time that I did not know, or that I did not think I knew, about the activities of those whose ranks I was so desperately anxious to join. I had decided in my own mind which of the publishing firms were on the up and up; and which were on the down and down. I sensed, or thought that I sensed, the policy underlying each individual list. Constable's, as I saw it, occupied a rather isolated, an idiosyncratic, niche in the publishing hierarchy. It was neither large, as publishing houses went, nor small. It was neither strident nor dim. Most Constable books maintained a high standard—but at any moment the firm might produce a popular best-seller. I had gained an impression that such occurrences were in the nature of happy accidents. I thought of Constable's as a quiet, distinguished and gentlemanly firm. If, by any remote chance, they could find a place for me, Constable's, I was convinced, would suit me very well indeed.

I found that Mr Kyllmann, when I went to see him, occupied a small office on the first floor. Most of the space in it was taken up by his desk, which was bare, swept and garnished, by a huge battered leather-covered armchair, a Victorian horsehair couch, and a green filing cabinet. Mr Kyllmann had very bright brown eyes, and a big lump on his upper lip that was only partially hidden by a bristly grey moustache. His conversation was disconcertingly punctuated by sudden snorts and grunts; and his manner was singularly unforthcoming. I did not realize, though I might have guessed, that he was a desperately shy man. He thought, though he was by no means sure, that there might be room in the firm for a learner. I told him that that was what I wanted to be. I also assured him that I was perfectly prepared to start right at the bottom. If necessary, I would be happy to lick stamps. No doubt a great many other young men had told him the same thing. While we talked, Mr Kyllmann smoked cigarette after cigarette, fitting them into a stained ivory holder. He kept his cigarettes, I noticed, in a battered green tin box. Just as there was nothing grand or flashy about the Constable premises, so there was nothing grand or flashy about this formally but untidily dressed elderly man. At one point in our interview he took a pinch of snuff, indulging thereafter in a Homeric bout of sneezing. Some of the snuff fell on to the grey woollen cardigan which, incongruously, he wore with a short black coat, striped trousers, and a blue and white spotted bow tie. He appeared to be pleased, and even a bit impressed, by the fact that I was on the staff of the Royal Institute of International Affairs. As I later discovered, the study of international affairs was, after Constable & Company, the main interest of his life.

If I joined his partner and himself—and he emphasized that the chances against this eventuality were pretty high—would I, he inquired, be in a position to invest money in the firm? I told him about the trustees; and he grunted ominously. There would be no question, he snapped, of any trustees ever seeing a Constable balance sheet. What he had in mind, he explained—what he had very vaguely at the back of his mind—was the possibility of my taking up some Constable debentures. I had only the haziest idea of what debenture shares were; but Mr Kyllmann spoke of them as if they were cast-iron securities which anyone in his right senses would be overjoyed to have the chance of acquiring. I said in a rush of optimism that I was quite sure that the trustees would be only too pleased to take up some Constable debentures. This enthusiasm, as I quickly saw, was a tactical mistake. Mr Kyllmann at once retreated into the innermost recesses of his shell. It was most improbable, he proceeded to tell me, that they would be able to find room for me. For one thing there was nowhere for me to sit. Wisely, I restrained an impulse to tell him that, if only he would allow me to come, I would gladly sit on the floor. "But since you are here," Mr Kyllmann grudgingly observed, "I suppose that I might as well take you in to see my partner, Sadleir."

I was very well aware that Michael Sadleir was a director of Constable's. I did not know at this time that he in fact held a controlling financial interest in the firm. Michael Sadleir was a member of my club. I had seen him there from time to time, but I had never spoken to him. He had struck me as an impressive-looking but rather unapproachable man. I should have liked to have made his acquaintance, for he was a distinguished writer as well as an active publisher—and that was exactly what I aspired to be myself. I congratulated myself on this chance of being introduced to him.

Mr Kyllmann led me out of his own office, along a dark narrow passage, and into Michael Sadleir's room. It was like entering another and quite different world. Whereas Mr Kyllmann's room had struck me as small and stuffy, Michael Sadleir's was large and airy. There had been a great many books in Mr Kyllmann's office, but they had had a dusty, unkempt, ill-arranged look. Ranged round the walls of Michael Sadleir's room there were elegant bookcases in which, behind glass, fine bindings gleamed. On the open shelves behind his big, cluttered desk there were neat rows of new or newish Constable books, pristine in their brightly coloured dust-jackets. On the walls of Mr Kyllmann's office I had noticed a few yellowing photographs of authors, a postcard from George Bernard Shaw framed in passe-partout, and a reproduction of an all-too-well-known painting by Van Gogh. On the primrose-yellow walls of Michael Sadleir's room—its ceiling was dashingly painted strawberry pink—there were colour prints of Victorian London, and one or two impressive-looking modern paintings.

Michael Sadleir was an exceptionally good-looking man. He must then have been in his late forties. He was tall, with wavy hair; and the double-breasted suits that he always wore without a waistcoat, though very well cut, were in some subtle way slightly unlike the ordinary run of double-breasted suits. He affected striped shirts and soft collars, rather striking ties, and suede shoes. He was for ever putting on, and taking off, a pair of spectacles with thin tortoiseshell rims. Mr Kyllmann favoured old-fashioned eyeglasses, attached to a black ribbon.

If his appearance and his surroundings suggested that Michael Sadleir's manner would be less gruff and abrupt than that of his

28

partner, I was fated, in the course of my first meeting with him, to be quickly disillusioned. Nothing could have been much gruffer or much more abrupt than our brief interview. Neither Mr Kyllmann nor I was invited to sit down. "This young man, Michael," Mr Kyllmann began, "seems to have the idea that he would like to join us as a learner." "Really?" Michael said; adding, as an afterthought, "Yes, I see." Standing at my side in front of Michael Sadleir's desk, Mr Kyllmann shuffled his feet uneasily. For some reason he had, as I had already noticed, undone the laces of his walking shoes. It gave him an oddly ramshackle air. "I have told him," Mr Kyllmann went on, "that we really have no room to take on anyone just for the present." Michael Sadleir agreed warmly. "Quite," he said. Then he added, "Of course, I suppose we might think about it?" "Think about it?" Mr Kyllmann echoed. "Oh, well, yes. I suppose we might." Michael Sadleir played with his spectacles, and turned over the sheet of paper on which he had been writing. I had hoped against hope that he might possibly have read one or other of my two novels. If he had, he made no allusion to either of them. Mr Kyllmann grunted, snuffled, and twirled his eye-glasses on the end of their ribbon. The interview was at an end.

Failing to realize that Michael Sadleir, too, was an unusually shy man, I naturally supposed that I had failed to find favour in his eyes. I expected to hear no more from Orange Street. But in the event I did. I received another stiff little note from Mr Kyllmann, asking me for the names and addresses of my mother's trustees. The senior trustee, in due course, received a still stiffer and still more uncompromising communication from Constable's chairman. Throughout the negotiations that ensued, these long-suffering trustees, as they frequently complained, were treated as if they had been defaulting debtors. Secretly, I think they were rather impressed by this novel approach. Once, greatly daring, I rang Mr Kyllmann up on the telephone. First, I had to speak to his secretary and factotum, Mr Bates. Mr Bates was a nervous, highly conscientious little man, one

29

of whose duties was to ascertain what any caller, rash enough to
ring up his master, might wish to say. On this occasion, after he
had conferred at length with the chairman on the internal
telephone, I was at last put through. The grunts, snuffles and
snorts, magnified by the instrument, were really terrifying.
Mr Kyllmann's replies were limited to "No," "Yes," and
"Possibly."

When the Arnold-Constable negotiations were in their final
phase I had an unnerving experience. For the first and, so far,
only time in my life I received an anonymous letter. Signed
"Wellwisher," it warned me against having anything to do with
Constable & Co. Its writer, or so he claimed, was deeply in-
debted to several members of my family for past kindnesses. He
could not stand by and watch me take a step which I should
inevitably regret. I have often wondered who wrote this letter;
and it now occurs to me that its author may well have been
Mr Kyllmann himself. Having committed himself thus far, it
would have been entirely in character if, at the last moment, he
had lost his nerve and had ardently desired to see and hear no
more of me.

Chapter Three

I SPENT the best part of four years in Orange Street, first as a "learner" and then as a kind of "perpetual apprentice." I was neither fish, fowl, nor good red herring. I suppose that at the back of everyone's mind there was an idea that I might one day become a director; but that goal, so far as I myself was concerned, seemed a very long way off. The heads of the various departments invariably treated me with great kindness, mixed with a faintly wary deference. This was partly due to innate good manners, and partly, I dare say, to a feeling that I was an embryo member of the Board.

I was given a rickety chair, and an equally rickety table, in the Production Manager's room. It was a small and very untidy office, cluttered up with old-fashioned wooden filing cabinets, dusty parcels of used blocks, bundles of galley proofs, stacks of page proofs bound in brown paper which no one in the end had wanted, and piles of imperfect copies which someone would one day do something about. The telephone on Mr Terry's crowded desk was always ringing. Charged with teaching me all he could about book production, fat efficient little Mr T. did his level best, explaining with the expert's baffling lack of clarity the processes with which he was perpetually involved. As he was doing the work of at least two men, and as nearly all his manifold jobs were of a highly technical nature, I was not unnaturally bamboozled and confused; and for a good deal of the time I was assigned tasks which were expressly designed to keep me quiet. So I endlessly copied out figures from invoices on to cost cards, or figures from delivery notes on to stock cards, welcoming frequent interruptions in the shape of visits from printers', binders', paper-makers', and block-makers' representatives.

These visits were conducted with as distinctive a ritual as that followed by courting birds. Before a hint of the real reason for the call could be mentioned, mutual inquiries about health had to be exchanged. Mr T. had various mild ailments; this representative suffered from asthma, that from indigestion. And quite often, in the background, there was a wife who had had a nasty operation, or a child or colleague who was in hospital. Then a little general conversation could be indulged in. The vagaries of the weather—which never failed to astound both parties—came in useful. They simply could not get over the fact that, in summer, it was sometimes quite hot, in winter very frequently cold, and that at all seasons of the year it often rained. After expressions of mutual astonishment and indignation had been exchanged, one further carefully chosen topic of more particular interest could be broached. It might be football in the winter, cricket in the summer. Occasionally a morsel of spicy trade gossip would be in order. Macmillan's, it might be revealed, had had a flop with a recent novel. They had printed ten thousand, bound seven five, and they had sold, to date, a measly twelve hundred. Such pieces of intelligence, especially if they referred to a highly successful firm like Macmillan's, made everyone feel a good deal happier. No one, they suggested, could be right all the time. Then, at long last, the reason for the call could be safely discussed. A manuscript could be handed over for cast-off and estimate. A date could be given, and argued about, for galley proofs. Designs for binding brasses could be discussed, book cloth specimen-books could be thumbed through and a colour chosen, and the story of fifty mislaid copies of this title or that pursued. An order for so many reams of such and such paper, weight so and so, could be given, with instructions as to where they were to be sent. And originals of book illustrations could be produced, and their sizing-up discussed.

Now and then, before taking his leave, one of these visitors would assume a serious expression, and would ask Mr Terry if he thought it would be possible for him to have just a word either with the head of the accounts department or with the chairman. When Mr Terry had done some telephoning, and when the emissary had departed, either downstairs to accounts or across the passage to Mr Kyllmann's room, Mr T. would make a clicking noise with his tongue, and I would be given to understand that the representative's firm was unhappy about the state of our account.

In this, and in a lot of other ways, I was made aware of the hard facts of economic life so far as publishing was concerned—not least by Mr Terry's own scrupulous care in saving pennies here and halfpennies there. Mr Sadleir, I was given to understand, could be wilfully and wildly extravagant; and the Old Gentleman, as Mr Kyllmann was always called in the office, had a passion for putting off paying accounts for as long as he possibly could. As I now realize, nearly all small and medium-sized publishing houses in the 1930s, and some of the big ones as well, were in pretty desperate financial straits. Some people said that the slump in book sales was due to the effects of the cinema and of wireless—people just did not read books any more. Others held that the book-buyers of the past had been badly hit by the economic depression. And there was all this uncertainty in the international field. Mr Terry, and the other heads of departments when they dropped into his room from time to time for little confidential chats, seemed inclined to blame the Constable directors; and I used to overhear such phrases as, "Now in the old days, when Mr Meredith and Mr Agnew were here . . ." "Living on our fat, that's what we're doing, and you mark my words, our back list is running down. . . ." "Queer street . . ."

These were gloomy prognostications, but they did not appear to be shared by the directors or, if they were, I was given no hint of it. From time to time the house telephone on Mr

T.'s desk would ring, and the chairman would announce that if it was convenient to Mr Terry and to myself he would be glad to have a word with me in his room. This meant that Mr Kyllmann had found himself with nothing to do, and was prepared to kill two birds with one stone—provide himself with a captive audience, and continue my education in the higher reaches of publishing practice. I would be told to sit in his leather armchair, I would be offered a cigarette from the battered green tin box, my state of health would be inquired into (the chairman was a mild health maniac), and a "little talk" would be launched from the text of some letter that had just come in, or from a set of figures which he had recently extracted from accounts or production. Inevitably, these sessions would end either with a flood of reminiscence or with a dissertation on the situation in Europe—what Freddie Voigt had told him that morning; what Arnold Wilson thought (Sir Arnold Wilson, then editor of the *Nineteenth Century*, had an office at the top of the house); or what Mr Stanley Baldwin had written in a recent letter to Miss Helen Waddell.

I was summoned much more rarely to Michael Sadleir's room—and then only when he had some small job that he wanted me to do; and whereas Mr Kyllmann was inevitably rambling and long-winded, Michael would be short, brusque and to the point. Mr Kyllmann would appear to have nothing in the world to do; Michael would invariably be in the middle of some herculean task. When I had been dismissed, Mr Kyllmann would ring with apparent reluctance for Mr Bates—he had evidently nerved himself to dictate a letter which, as I knew, involved the muttering and mumbling of some complicated rigmarole which his patient factotum would put into reasonable shape. Michael, when I got up to go, would return thankfully to the job he had in hand. He was accustomed, I was aware, to have long dictating sessions with his secretary, when he could sometimes be glimpsed through the half-open door of his office, pacing the carpet and intoning in a loud, confident voice.

Michael never made the slightest conscious attempt to teach me anything. Either, I decided, he had made up his mind that I would never be any good and that it would be a waste of his time; or, more simply, that he could not be bothered. I was almost certainly wrong on both counts. He was, in fact, ridiculously, even morbidly, modest and diffident; and I genuinely believe that he genuinely believed that he possessed no publishing knowledge that was worth passing on to anyone. Mr Kyllmann had no such inhibitions.

If I have given the idea that life in Orange Street at this time was rather grim—grumbling hands at the pumps of a foundering ship, cursing the captain and officers for their inefficiency—I have given a totally wrong impression. Grumbling was occasional and sporadic—for one thing the senior members of the staff, those admirable old family servants with the virtues and failings of their kind, were desperately busy, and had very little time in which to indulge in luxuries of this nature. I can appreciate now how grossly over-worked they were, and what prodigies they performed. And then, too, despite anything they might say, they were, to a man, devoted to the firm. Its fortunes were their fortunes, its fate their fate.

Constable & Company, as I very soon discovered, had a strangely endearing *persona*. This stemmed partly, I imagine, from tradition, partly from the personalities of its directors, and partly from these same senior members of its staff, most of whom had been with the firm since the time they had left school. Although no members of the "founding family" remained, Constable's was very much a family concern, revolving round the moods of its directors. If they were in a good mood, all was sweetness and light. If they were in a bad mood a gloom descended. But everyone was used to that; and accepted it.

Mr Kyllmann could be, and quite often was, difficult, inconsiderate, unpredictable and monumentally selfish; but he was admired, liked and respected partly because he was a "character," partly because he was recognized as a thorough-paced professional, who knew the business of publishing from A to Z, partly because he had, behind him, some glittering and solid successes, and partly because he could be, all of a sudden, extraordinarily kind and rather endearing. Michael Sadleir could be, and often was, detached, aloof, unpredictable and, to all appearances, wildly and irresponsibly extravagant—scrapping a whole set of wrapper blocks, for example, at the last moment because he had suddenly had a belated and better idea. But he was liked, admired and respected because he was so obviously a man of real distinction, because the firm basked in the reflected glory of his success as a writer, a bibliographer, a collector and a bookman, because he had great charm, and because he was recognized as possessing a genuine and exciting publishing flair. He could also be, and often was, astonishingly generous in an off-hand, slightly embarrassed kind of way; and although he sometimes did wild things that cost Constable's a lot of money, he was very far from being a dilettante. Which in a sense was rather remarkable. He was known, or thought, to have very considerable private means—to be a very rich man. Publishing for him, it was supposed, was simply a hobby; and under these circumstances it might have been expected that he would have shirked tedious, fiddling jobs, and would have been bored with petty detail. But not at all. Within the field of his publishing operations—and it was a limited field—he was one of the most meticulously careful and conscientious men I have ever worked for. He fussed endlessly about small things—doing up parcels, posting letters, and saving pieces of string and sheets of brown paper. And he was every bit as careful about more important matters like manuscripts and proofs. Martha Smith, the third director, could be, and often was, a bit fault-finding and (as we were pleased to think) bossy—which, after all, was her job; but she was respected because it was recognized that she worked like a Trojan, because she provided a much needed element of sheer horse-trading common sense on the Board, because she and she alone, as it was believed, could curb Michael's wilder flights of extravagance, and because quite often she would shed her disapproving attitude, and be as nice as she could be—which was very nice indeed. She, too, had great charm, a first-rate, quick brain, and a cynical wit.

And then, too, as publishers, though the firm might be chronically short of money, Constable's was very far from being unsuccessful. We published a lot of good and a lot of successful books in the 1930s, as well as plenty of unsuccessful ones; and in publishing there is always a winner just round the corner. This title may have been a complete flop, and that one a sad disappointment. But the books coming out next week are bound to do outstandingly well.

The two super-optimists in the firm were Mr Kyllmann and Ernie Vines, our town traveller. Very often, when a mint new book from the first binders' parcel to be opened was placed on the chairman's desk, he would summon me to his room. On these occasions Mr Terry would groan, for it was a standing joke that any copy of a new Constable book that was given to Mr Kyllmann would as sure as eggs are eggs turn out to be imperfect. A signature would be missing or out of its proper order, or would have been bound in upside down. But, if all was well, I would find the old boy handling what might well be a quite undistinguished novel with a kind of joyful reverence, his brown eyes gleaming with genuine enthusiasm. It was extremely unlikely that he had read the book in question, either when it had come in as a manuscript or at the proof stage. It was extremely unlikely, in point of fact, that he would ever read it. But he had, as he would proudly tell me, "glanced at the first few pages." "Excellent," he would say. "First class. The author is just a slip of a girl, or so Michael tells me. In some ways she reminds me of dear Edith Wharton. The way she puts her sentences together, don't you know. Vines is expecting great things in the way of sales."

That went without saying. Ernie Vines, a former amateur

footballer of note, not only said that he expected great things from every new Constable book that he subscribed to the booksellers, he actually believed what he said. He could talk the hind-leg off a horse, and could persuade a London bookseller who did not want to take a book at all to order six copies firm, and six on sale. Publishers' representatives—the commercial travellers of the book trade—are important people, and there is a popular theory nowadays that they should not be over-persuasive. "It's no good," the argument runs, "sticking a bookseller with a book he won't be able to sell. If he wants to pass a title, let him pass it. Or next time, when you've got something really good to offer, he'll be shy, and with good reason." Whenever I hear this sensible doctrine I think of Ernie Vines. He would have laughed it to scorn. He believed that if a bookseller could be browbeaten into taking a decent number of *any* title, nine times out of ten he would contrive to sell every copy he had bought. And he would not have sold them if they had not been in his shop.

I learnt all that I ever knew about the practical side of book production from Mr Terry, and from the three months that I spent at the Whitefriars Press at Tonbridge, a firm that did a good deal of printing for us. I thought that I was going to enjoy this summer interlude very much indeed, for I would live at home and drive over to Tonbridge every day. In fact I found my initiation into the mysteries of printing both boring and physically exhausting.

For one thing I was incapable of understanding machinery which, owing to trade union regulations, I was never, probably fortunately, allowed to operate. So I had to stand for hours on end watching printing presses revolving at varying speeds. I was given, it is true, some old type, and was allowed to stand in a corner and set up a page of the *Nineteenth Century*, but no sooner had I got the thing almost finished than as sure as fate I would drop it, and would have to begin all over again. Any dreams I had harboured of installing a private printing press in my stables and of producing exquisite hand-set and hand-printed books—The Meadow House Press—quickly evaporated. But I did learn how books were actually printed; I learnt the language of printing; I at one time knew, or thought I knew, all about impositions, paper, and printing inks; and I developed an enthusiasm, which has never quite left me, for type-faces. In my hey-day I could go through the publishers' advertisement columns of the *Sunday Times* and identify every single type-face that had been used.

My spell at the Whitefriars Press was physically exhausting because, in a printing works, no one but the key-board operators ever sits down. There is nowhere to sit. So, for hours on end, I stood on a concrete floor—and very tiring I found it. I used to dread the prospect of another day of inaction and aching legs; and in order to provide a little variety in this dismal round I very often used to drive in to Tonbridge not in our current car, but in my bull-nosed Morris Cowley. This veteran dated from the early 1920s, and had a rather romantic history.

Shortly before I had got engaged to be married, an event which coincided with my arrival at Orange Street, I had gone with a party that included my wife-to-be to the Ile de Porquerolles, off Hyères; and one night when I was there I had had a remarkable dream. I dreamt that on my return I was met at Dover by my mother who told me that a cousin of my father's had died, and had left him his house, called Balloon Hall, and all its contents. I remember thinking when I woke up that this was a very odd name for a house; and wishing that it could be true and not just a dream, because I was already contemplating matrimony and some furniture would come in handy. When I got back to England I was duly met by my mother who told me that a cousin of my father's, of whose existence I was unaware, had in fact died while I had been abroad, and had left him his house, which was called Blaby Hall, and everything in it. We hurried up to Leicestershire to examine this new possession. It was an eerie experience. The cousin in question had been a life-long bachelor who, when he was at Oxford, had had an unfortunate accident in a dog-cart. An only child, he had lived with his mother at Blaby; and after she had died at a ripe old age he had gone to pieces. For years he had never left the grounds; and he had done his best to drink himself to death. Some distressing things had happened. Going up to bed one night in a state of intoxication he had fallen down, and the candle he had been carrying had gouged out one of his eyes. The carpet in his dining-room was a sea of grease. Food had bored him, and he had been accustomed to throw his breakfasts, lunches and dinners on to the floor for the delectation of his innumerable small white dogs. The house was stuffed with furniture and pictures, some good, some bad. It was a kind of nightmare Aladdin's cave. I remember opening a drawer in a desk and finding in it old photographs, locks of hair, each neatly labelled, and a large diamond ring. In the coach-house I discovered the old Morris Cowley two-seater. His master had bought it, the gardener told me, soon after the First World War, but had hardly ever taken it out. Its speedometer registered six hundred miles. I had been allowed to keep it. It buzzed along in a most cheerful way, and driving it cheered up those dismal daily pilgrimages.

I doubt if I ever made much practical use of what I had learnt at Tonbridge, but I enjoyed, on my return to Orange Street, designing title-pages, laying out text pages, and devising a new style for Constable's advertisements. These activities led me into conflict with Mr Kyllmann, Michael Sadleir, and Martha Smith.

The Old Gentleman, if he caught me devising an elaborate layout for a manuscript that was going off to the printer's, was apt to be indignant. What, he demanded, were printers for if they could not devise a decent title-page and a decent text-page themselves? Employ a good printer, and leave all that nonsense to him. I was wasting my own time and the time of the firm. Michael had a rather different outlook. For a book in which he was interested he was far from willing to leave everything to the printer. Instead he would produce a layout of his own. It would arrive in due course on Mr Terry's desk; and I would regard it with horror. A layout, I was convinced, should be a meticulously neat affair, with ruled pages, headings skilfully simulating the type in which they were to be set, and endless minutely written instructions. Michael's were scrawled monstrosities, laundry-list affairs jotted down on any odd scrap of paper, with jumbled lines and arrows and a few semi-legible observations. Occasionally I would attempt to reduce one of these nightmares to some kind of order. This, when it was discovered, caused resentment. And with good reason. Although Michael had no expert knowledge of typography, he knew exactly what he wanted, and he had an amateur's flair for achieving it. His untidy layouts invariably produced much more satisfactory results then my painstakingly careful ones.

Martha Smith was responsible for Constable's advertising. In the flush of my new-found expertise I had decided, on heaven knows what inadequate grounds, that the layouts of her advertising copy were old-fashioned. I suppose that I must have said as much. One answer might have been—"Well, if you don't like them, try to produce something better yourself." But I was far too junior to be allowed to do anything of the kind; and for a time there was a state of undeclared war between us. It was a one-sided campaign, for she had an all-round superiority in armaments.

One day I was told by Michael that I had better attend the Wednesday afternoon manuscript meetings. This I regarded as promotion, and I used to look forward to Wednesday as the highspot of the week. At these ritual gatherings I felt that I was approaching the beating heart of the firm. The Wednesday meetings could also be extremely entertaining. Present in the boardroom on these occasions were the three directors, Mr Looker (the firm's Reader), an outside "adviser" if there happened to be one at the moment, David Grover, who looked after our technical books, and myself.

I was, and still am, deeply attached to Sammy Looker, who had originally been recruited to the firm in 1923—on a three months' trial. A small man with a beard, he occupied a horrid little den right at the top of the house; and he spent his laborious days reading the manuscripts that had been sent in to us. If a new book from a Constable author, or a manuscript about which something was known, arrived, it would probably be read first by one of the directors. But the bulk of the offerings that came in week by week went to Sammy, who acted as a kind of literary sieve. Sammy Looker, to my mind, was and is one of the most complete "bookmen" I have ever known. He loved books as such—he used to spend most of his lunch-hours treasure-trove hunting in the Charing Cross Road. He had a great knowledge of books—he would have made an admirable antiquarian bookseller. He had a life-long interest in Richard Jefferies. He collected his manuscripts, many of them unpublished, and edited a series of books on Jefferies's writing and notebooks. And he was a first-class judge of contemporary writing. In the course of his work at Constable's he must have read thousands of manuscripts, most of them worthless. About each he typed a sensible, succinct report, though he was no typist. He never lost his enthusiasm. His reward, the only reward for which he asked, was the discovery, just now and again, of a genuine new talent. Such discoveries really did excite him. He was implicitly trusted. Michael was devoted to him—one bookman recognized another; but he used to rag him unmercifully. There was a theory that, in the intervals of his mammoth bouts of reading, Sammy used to cook kippers on a gas stove in his stuffy little office.

42

"You can always tell when a manuscript has been through Sammy's hands," Michael used to say, "because the pages will be stuck down with horrid little bits of fish." Mr Kyllmann used to plague Sammy's life by constantly sending for him. The Old Gentleman insisted that all the parcels that came in to Constable's should be taken straight up to his room. He would there and then undo each package as it arrived and, if it contained a manuscript, he would ring for Sammy. Sometimes Sammy would have to toil up and down the stairs four or five times in a single morning. In matters of this kind Mr Kyllmann was curiously inconsiderate.

The "outside advisers" used to come and go. Mr Kyllmann once imported a publicity expert in whom, for a very short time, he placed absolute faith; but generally the purpose of these experts was to assist Constable's to get the right kind of new books. Each, to begin with, was assumed to be an answer to prayer. He knew all the young writers. He attended all the literary bun-fights. He knew the younger book critics. He was hand-in-glove with the smaller agents who were beginning to handle some promising manuscripts. He knew what was going on in other publishing houses. He would get Constable's the fast-selling books that were needed. He would be a breath of fresh air, a tonic, a shot in the arm. One was excellent, and lasted a long time.

A rigid protocol obtained at these Wednesday afternoon manuscript meetings. Mr Kyllmann sat at the head of the table and Michael at its foot. Martha sat entrenched behind a large black notebook, known as the Bible, in which decisions were recorded. Sammy Looker presided over a side table stacked with tottering piles of manuscripts—manuscripts in coloured folders with neat labels, manuscripts encased in formidable spring-back binders, and manuscripts which were untidy faggots of typescript, precariously secured with string or tape. "Manuscripts with reports" were taken first, "first report" manuscripts getting priority. The manuscript itself would be handed to the

43

Old Gentleman, the report to Michael. Mr Kyllmann would first balance the offering in his hand; and then open it, peering and snuffling suspiciously at a page here and a page there. While this was going on—and there was a vague superstition that thanks to long practice the Chairman could in fact divine by feel and smell whether the thing was going to be any good or not—Michael would read the report in his clear, pleasing voice. He read extremely well, and to his eternal credit he always took just as much trouble with reports that began "This is a worthless piece of work, fit only for a third- or fourth-rate list," as he did with ones that started, "I should certainly recommend a second reading of what I believe to be, in its way, an outstanding piece of work." Optimistic reports of that kind were few and far between; and the first part of the meeting usually went swimmingly, with the pile of "rejects" on the floor beside Sammy's chair growing higher and higher. It was when we came to manuscripts with second, third, fourth and even fifth reports that trouble was likely to start.

It always amazed me that Michael did not assume quasi-dictorial powers in the matter of what manuscripts we should accept. When I first attended manuscript meetings he was, unquestionably, at the height of his very considerable powers. As a young man he had gone through an *avant-garde* phase, when only the *outré* or the extreme had excited his admiration. After that, though his taste was often a bit in advance of that of the great British reading public, he came to exercise a judicious balance between what he himself liked and what would be generally acceptable. He had his hates—anything that seemed to him dull, stodgy, or unadventurous; and this had led him to be a pioneer of the more advanced American novel. Some of the American writers whom Constable's published in the 1920s and '30s sold well—others were before their time. Occasionally he would mistake a goose for a swan, but such mistakes were few and far between. And his fondness for adventurous writing never blinded him to the quality of smaller, stiller voices, if

44

these voices were really worth listening to. He was a very sound judge of a book.

With the insight that I later obtained, I can now think of three good reasons why Michael refrained so assiduously from laying down the law. The first reason was his genuine modesty. He was convinced that no one man's judgement is infallible; and he once told me that dictator-publishers should remember that while the public's taste changed, their own likes and dislikes generally remained pretty static. The second reason was that he rather enjoyed the weekly manuscript meetings; and he probably felt that there would be little point in holding them if he invariably took all the decisions. And the third reason was that he hated rows.

Occasionally he would say in one of his reports—which were always clear, logical, penetrating and often very funny—"This is an excellent piece of work, which we must certainly publish." And Mr Kyllmann always unhesitatingly accepted such a verdict—as well he might. But such occasions were rare. Much more often he would say, in effect, "I like this book very much, but before we decide to take it we must have some other opinions."

This practice resulted in a multiplicity of reports, which could produce muddles; and it sometimes resulted in our accepting books which we would have been better without. If someone else—so long as it was not himself—had cracked up a manuscript which Michael, when he had got round to reading it, had disliked, I used to think it would have been sounder policy if it had been turned down then and there. But no. It was only Michael's view against another reader's; and the manuscript must be handed on to someone else.

He was prepared to take a lot of trouble to avoid a row. One of us might have championed a manuscript, quite possibly exaggerating its virtues in our enthusiasm. Michael, if he had not liked it, never failed to say so in his report; but he was always anxious to avoid getting embroiled in an argument which might become heated. In cases like these, "getting further opinions" was an easy way out.

If he was in a good mood—and this happened more often than not—Mr Kyllmann was a distinct asset at a manuscript meeting. He could be wise, delightful and, in his own way, amusing. He was an excellent raconteur. If he happened to be in a bad mood, he could be absolutely maddening—wilfully muddling one book up with another, and pulling all his many prejudices out of the bag, one after the other. It used to puzzle me why he read so little, for he had a genuine love and appreciation of good writing, and when he did read a manuscript—and this happened only once in a blue moon—his criticisms were well-founded, acute and remarkably perceptive. I imagine that he had read so much in his day that he had got bored with the process, and found it a strain. Martha Smith read a good many novels in manuscript and, on the whole, was generally inclined to come down on the "rejecting" side of the fence. If she had had her way, I used to think, we should have published very few books indeed. Often enough, time proved her to have been right. Sometimes, if there was a manuscript that I had liked and that she had subsequently read, her objections enraged me—I suspected, quite unjustly, that she had been prejudiced by some completely irrelevant issue.

After we had dealt with all the manuscripts with reports, we tackled "the new manuscripts"—manuscripts which had come in since the previous Wednesday. Each in turn was passed to the Chairman who duly handled, weighed, peered and sniffed at it; while the letter that had come with it was read aloud by Michael. These letters were rather fun. Some authors, in submitting their wares, displayed a due and proper modesty. Others informed us, in no uncertain terms, that if we turned their books down we should be fools or worse. Covering letters from literary agents were red rags to a bull so far as Mr Kyllmann was concerned. With a very few exceptions he hated literary agents, maintaining that they interposed an unnecessary and undesirable

46

barrier between author and publisher. And there had been one famous occasion when an agent had written to his favourite author (addressing the letter to her c/o Constable's) suggesting that if she would allow him to handle her literary affairs he was confident that he could obtain far better terms either from her present publishers or from some other, more enterprising firm. In accordance with this lady's own standing instructions, all letters sent to her at Orange Street were opened by Mr Kyllmann. He had opened this one. The fat had been fairly in the fire; and the agent, summoned peremptorily into his presence, must have spent an uncomfortable quarter of an hour.

Most agents, knowing how the land lay, wrote to Michael. But occasionally an unwary one would write to Mr Kyllmann. Such letters afforded Michael great satisfaction, and he would read them out with gusto. " 'My dear Kyllmann,' " he would start, to be stopped by a snort of indignation from the Chairman. "I am *not* 'his dear Kyllmann'," the Old Gentleman would announce crossly. "I hardly know the fellow. I doubt if I should recognize him if I met him in the street. 'Dear Mr Kyllmann' if he must; but 'Dear Sir' would be more fitting. These people have no manners. But go on, my dear Michael, go on, and let us hear what he has to say." " 'I am delighted,' " Michael would continue, peering impishly over the top of his spectacles, " 'to be able to give you the *first*'—first underlined —'offer of British Empire rights in a novel which will, unless I am very much mistaken, be right down your street.' " " *Right down my street*?" The Chairman's voice would be hoarse with indignation. " 'Right down my street'? What a quite extraordinary expression. What on earth can the silly fellow mean? Really, I must write and tell him to stop sending me foolish letters like this—or Bates must write. Remind me, my dear Arnold, after the meeting, to give little Bates a note to that effect. And now let us quickly pass on to something else." The unoffending manuscript, which had had such an unfortunate introduction, would be handed to Sammy, who received the bulk of the new manuscripts. Michael generally took a couple every week, and Martha and the "adviser" and I would get our quota.

One thing is certain. Our elaborate and cumbersome procedure ensured that any author who submitted his work to Constable's could be certain of getting a scrupulously fair deal. I do not think that, taken by and large, it was a bad method of dealing with manuscripts.

I used to read manuscripts at the week-ends; but, unlike Charlie Evans, I never spent Saturdays in bed. Indeed, in those days, the office functioned on Saturday mornings. One Saturday I turned up wearing grey flannel trousers and a tweed coat. Summoned unexpectedly to the Old Gentleman's room, he looked me up and down with distaste. "We are not on the golf links now, you know," he told me.

In addition to the weekly manuscript meetings and Mr Kyllmann's frequent "little talks," I gained a certain amount of experience in the wider aspects of the art and practice of publishing. Now and then, if one of our travellers was ill, I would be sent out on the road to subscribe our forthcoming books. Fighting down a tendency warmly to agree with booksellers when they looked at one of our new books and said, "Very nice. But who is going to buy it?" I tried hard to emulate the tactics of the ebullient Ernie Vines. But I lacked his self-confidence. Then I was for ever being sent off to look for material for book illustrations. I remember going to a ramshackle house in Kensington that was filled from cellar to attics with Victorian prints and daguerreotype photographs. "A lot of junk, if you ask me," the caretaker assured me. "You could have the whole boiling if you offered a hundred quid." It would have been a sound investment.

I was sent down on one occasion to Hove to intercede with Lord Alfred Douglas. We were bringing out Frank Harris's *Oscar Wilde*, with an Introduction by Bernard Shaw; and Lord

48

Alfred, who had got hold of a proof, wrote in to say that unless we deleted certain passages he would sue us for libel. I do not recall what I had expected, but I found a wizened little old man in a small and desperately shabby flat. He was evidently very hard up. He could not have treated me with more kindness; and he agreed to a minimum of alteration to the text of the book. So I thought that all libel-threateners were easy money, until I was despatched to tackle the angry governess. We were publishing the reminiscences of a girl—aged about twelve—who had been born and brought up in a historic and extremely beautiful house. She had written her life story in an exercise book, adorning it with illustrations; and the whole thing was being reproduced in facsimile. An expensive venture, but the child wrote well and had a vivid imagination—and we thought that it might catch on. In one or two passages the author had adversely criticized her governess; and at some stage in the course of the book's production this point had been raised with her mother. These passages, it was pointed out, might be construed as libellous. Our fears had been laughed to scorn. "Oh, darling old So-and-so," we had been told. "Why, she's been with us for years. She really *is* one of the family. Of course she won't mind—in fact she'll be tremendously amused." But Miss So-and-so, when she had been given an advance copy of her pupil's book, had not been amused at all. She was justifiably quite cross, and her solicitors wrote us a sharp letter saying that their client's professional ability had been impugned, and that if the book came out containing the passages to which she took exception an action for libel would follow. I was told to go down to see what I could do—printing and inserting cancel pages would, at this late hour, be an expensive business. I spent a difficult and embarrassing day. Miss So-and-so was still with the family; and I had to interview in turn the author's mother, who persisted in her attitude of pooh-poohing the whole affair; the author who said, "But if what I said is true, why should it be changed?"; and then the governess herself—

who was charming. But she was also firm, and I could not help seeing her point.

At the time, I regarded being sent on missions of this kind as a mark of signal confidence in my ability. I realize now that if I had not been there to send, no one would have gone. Instead there would have been an unsatisfactory exchange of cross letters.

To say that someone is a bundle of contradictions is a pretty trite observation; but that was how Mr Kyllmann, Michael Sadleir, and Martha Smith each appeared to their "learner." I never knew—from one day to the next, and even from one hour to the next—how any of them would react to any given situation; and my doubts were shared by the other members of the staff. We were all kept well and truly on the hop. They had one thing in common. They all three loathed inefficiency and bungling. But beyond that, everything was one large question mark—depending on the mood that each of them happened to be in. I imagined that they reacted very strongly against one another; and I suspected that there were sometimes violent clashes of temperament. If Mr Kyllmann was in a good mood, he would treat me as an affectionate father might treat his favourite son; if he was in a bad mood he would treat me with icy contempt. Something had gone wrong—but I never knew what. Michael might call me in to his room to introduce me to a favourite author—and he would be in tremendous form, laughing about "Old Fishing Boots," as he always called Neville Chamberlain, and joking about the Chairman's pre-occupation with international affairs. An hour later, encounter-ing him again, he would be curt and snubbing. I had no idea why.

The whole atmosphere of the office depended on these moods. Sometimes one or other of the directors would fairly get their knife into a member of the staff. Then it was probably finish. He or she had done something, or said something, or had behaved in some way, that was unforgivable. From my lowly

50

observation post I fancied that none of the three was prepared to take a firm stand against the other two. I had many unhappy and uneasy days myself—for I was determined to stay on my slippery saddle if I could. But, looking back, I fancy that I enjoyed myself quite a lot in Orange Street. Mr Kyllmann was like a cross old dog—I was flattered and pleased when he wagged his tail at me. And Michael, in a good mood, was everything that I thought a distinguished writer-cum-publisher ought to be.

In the spring of 1939 there was an idea that I might take over Constable's "technical list" as a separate enterprise. This seems to me, in retrospect, to have been an unusually silly idea—for I knew next to nothing about technical publishing. But in any case the protracted negotiations to this end lasted right through that summer; and when the war broke out in September I was still a learner.

Chapter Four

I HAD made up my mind not to go back to publishing at the end of the war for a number of good and bad reasons. First and foremost, I was extremely doubtful if there would be a place for me in Orange Street; and in the improbable event of Constable's wanting me back, I was pretty sure that I did not want to go. Quite apart from the fact that, for reasons which I shall presently relate, I was feeling distinctly sore with both Michael and Mr Kyllmann, I felt that I ought to feel that it would be a mistake to settle down again in the old familiar rut. There were now, I thought, other and possibly more exciting things that I could perhaps do—though I was uncertain what those things might be.

At the back of my mind I realized that, in some ways, I was a more mature person than I had been in 1939. And I had a better opinion of myself. This did not mean—or I hope it did not mean—that I was pleased with myself, or cocksure. It did mean that I no longer imagined that almost everyone else in the world had much more ability than I possessed. During the course of the war I had contrived to hold down some un-bellicose but quite responsible posts.* My initial lack of confidence had made the process fairly hair-raising; but these experiences had taught me that other people were not so over-

* I wrote an account of my experiences between 1939 and 1945 in a book called *A Very Quiet War*, published in 1962. I was afraid that a lot of reviewers would feel impelled to observe that while brave men were risking their lives on various fronts and at sea, I swanned round in Rolls-Royces, and grumbled about the number of dinner parties that I had to go to in Delhi and Kandy. In the event, there were only a few notices of this kind—for which I was immensely grateful.

poweringly efficient as I had once imagined. Now, as I saw it in my more optimistic moments, there was no reason why, within reasonable bounds, I should not make a fair success of anything I tackled.

And then again, as always, there was this infernal itch to write. During the war, my views about writing had also changed. Of actual writing I had done very little—a handful of magazine short stories while I was with 12 Corps and Scottish Command; and some factual reporting while I was in Scotland and in the Far East. But I had lived a part of the time in close contact with a (to me) new breed of writer—journalists, some of whom had been first-class practitioners. Observing their methods, and listening to their talk, had convinced me of two things. Writing of any kind was a much more difficult art than I, in my blissful ignorance, had ever supposed. And while success in writing depended to a vital extent on "inspiration," or on having something worthwhile to say, it also depended to a very large extent on sheer hard work. Before, while I had been genuinely diffident in most other directions, I had been danger-ously and vaingloriously self-confident about writing. Provided I could think of something to write about, the rest, I had thought, was a piece of cake. And whereas I had worried madly about a lot of things, I had imagined that writing was almost as easy, and almost as automatic, as breathing.

Up to a certain point, my magazine story efforts during the early part of the war had also taught me a salutary lesson. Each story, it is true, had started with an idea—a flash of inspiration, if you like; only that is much too grand a word. But most of them had been detective stories, and these I had worked out in advance, not by a process of hard, concentrated, ice-cold thought —I was incapable of that—but at least by a process of jerky, spasmodic, spaced-out, fumbling cogitation. And that had at least been an improvement on my former method of getting an idea and then sitting down and writing with no notion of where I was going or what was going to happen. At the start of one of my detective stories I had known—I had had to know—how the thing would begin; I had generally had a ready-made central incident; and I had known how it would end. One example will show how the process worked.

When I was ADC to the GOC-in-C, Scottish Command, we stayed a night at Crathes Castle, in Aberdeenshire. Before dinner, we were shown round the gardens by our host and hostess. It was apparent that gardening was Sir James Burnett's ruling passion, and that Lady Burnett was equally enthusiastic and equally skilled. Even in wartime the gardens were quite lovely, and I particularly remember a long border that was filled exclusively with white-flowering plants. Driving back next morning to Edinburgh, my General happened to remark that of course our host was "garden mad." The phrase stuck in my mind; and that night in bed, before I went to sleep, I began to play with the idea of writing a story about a man who really and literally *was* "garden mad." What form would his madness take? He would stick at nothing, I decided, to make his garden as perfect as possible—better than those of any of his hated rivals. "Sticking at nothing," in the kind of short stories that I usually wrote, generally meant committing a murder. But how would committing a murder help him to achieve a super-excellent garden? Then I recalled Lady Burnett's expertise, and I remembered wondering at the time how great a part she had played in the perfection of the Crathes gardens. Suppose, for argument's sake, that the central character in my story was not, himself, a particularly skilled gardener? That could make him all the more greedy for success. And suppose he relied almost entirely on the skill of his wife? By the time I fell asleep I had arrived at a situation where my garden-mad hero could be made to murder wife after wife—as frequently, in fact, as he met an unmarried lady who seemed to promise better gardening results than the wife he possessed at the moment.

Reviewed while I was shaving next morning, this idea did not sound very convincing, so I put it into cold storage at the back of my mind. A few weeks later we spent a night at Loch-inch, where the gardens were bigger and grander but, I thought, not quite so lovely as those at Crathes. At Lochinch there was a heather garden, a lily garden, a quarry garden, and a rose garden. There was also a very large lake. "Jolly lucky for you," the General said to Lord Stair as he was showing us round, "that there isn't a target of military importance anywhere near. If there was, I should order you to drain that lake. Too good a guide to enemy aircraft." Lord Stair regarded his sheet of water with a puzzled frown. For a moment I fancied that he might be piqued that he himself was not regarded by General Thorne as a worth-while target. Then he spoke. "If the lake *was* drained," he said thoughtfully, "one could grow the most wonderful primulas in the sludge." A penny dropped. My "garden-mad" character would be a fantasticated version of this Scottish grandee. No great gardener himself—he would differ in this, as in many other respects, from Lord Stair—he would possess a world-famous heather garden, a world-famous lily garden, a world-famous quarry garden, and a world-famous rose garden. He would also possess a large lake. And he would have had four wives. Wife number one would have been an expert on *ericas*. The heather garden having been completed under her guidance and direction, and the garden-owner having met a lily expert, the *erica* expert would have been bumped off, and the construc-tion of a lily garden would have followed hard on the heels of his second marriage. Wife number two would have been elimin-ated as soon as the lily garden had been finished, and after an outstanding authority on alpines had been encountered; and this unlucky plantswoman would have disappeared in her turn as soon as the quarry garden had been well established and her husband had fallen in with a rose-grower with an international reputation. The lake would provide the climax. My garden-mad hero would suddenly be ordered to drain his lake—a wartime security measure—and in a flash he would see the possibilities of this muddy bottom for growing primulas. This would be the rose-expert wife's death sentence, for now he would have to find, and marry, a prominent primula fancier. At last, I thought, I had something to work on.

Next morning, while I was dressing in my Lochinch bedroom, I had another idea. The lake must, from the start, figure prominently in the story. *Ergo*—the garden-mad husband would have drowned each successive wife in it. A bathing accident, a boating accident, a quasi-accidental slither from its bank—the changes could be easily rung. And, on our way back to Edinburgh later that same morning, just as we passed a row of white-harled cottages which I can see clearly in my mind's eye to this very day, the twist that is so essential in a story of this kind occurred to me. Of course—Henry VIII. It was a Henry VIII kind of a story—and in a Henry VIII kind of a story the last wife must survive her husband. This by rights should have been the primula-fancier; but with too many successive wives the thing would be in danger of getting out of hand. Very well, then. The rose-expert would have to be the one to escape a watery death. But why? And how?

I must have been a dull and silent companion as we tore in our battleship-grey Rolls-Royce along the dreary main road between Glasgow and Edinburgh, for I was wrestling with my ridiculous problem. The solution dawned on me as we turned in at the Gogar Bank drive gates. The rose-wife, her task with the rose-garden completed, must suddenly tumble to what had happened to all her predecessors. She would realize that her own days were numbered, a conviction that would be strengthened when her husband announced that he had met a delightful Miss Somebody, whom he had asked to stay. Miss Somebody, he would explain, knew everything that there was to be known about the laying-out and planting of *potagers*. Would it not be delightful—and a real act of patriotism in the middle of a world war—to have an exquisite, decorative and productive vegetable garden *à la française*? The doomed rose-wive would do some fast thinking. In addition to her extensive

56

knowledge of roses, she was also pretty sound on primulas. Regarding the lake with a speculative eye—after all, unless she acted quickly, it would soon provide her with a speedy death— she has an inspiration. Miss Somebody arrives, bringing with her some mouth-watering plans and designs. The garden-mad husband's eyes kindle ominously. He proposes a boating picnic on the lake for the following afternoon. Next morning, just before luncheon, and after Miss Somebody has made her preliminary reconnaissance, the rose-wife takes her husband by the arm.

"You know, dearest, the picnic on the lake that you had planned for this afternoon?"

"I am eagerly looking forward to it."

"I do not think that you have been on the south terrace today?"

"No. Miss Somebody and I were busy in the walled garden."

"Then come with me. There is something I would like to show you."

Where the lake had been, there is now a great expanse of black mud, in which men are still working, cutting ditches to carry off the few remaining pools of water.

"Everyone," the rose-wife explains, "is being urged to drain lakes. They afford such excellent landmarks for enemy aircraft. So I arranged to have ours done as a surprise. Have they not been quick? You aren't angry, are you, dearest?"

"Of course not."

"Disappointed about the picnic?"

"No."

Her husband, she notes with delight, is peering down at the emptied lake with an expression of strained intensity. A gleam of mad enthusiasm comes into his eyes.

"That sludge."

"I know."

"A bog garden."

"Exactly. My beloved primulas."

"*Farinosa. Rosea. Auchterarderea.* You could do it, my dear. I really believe you could."

"I know I could." She looks speculatively at her husband, an elderly man. "Mind you," she says, "it will be a long job— ten years, fifteen years?"

When I came to write this story, I realized that there ought to be a narrator who witnessed the events leading up to the climax; so I invented a nervous little nursery-gardener, who had been invited to stay in order to see the gardens for which he had supplied many of the plants. The story got itself written in such spare time as I had.

All this, of course, was water under long-receded bridges; but could I, I wondered, now that I had supposedly evolved some kind of a technique for working out plots in advance, and now that I had allegedly seen the light in the matter of regarding writing as a hard, exacting chore, make a reasonable career, and a reasonably good living, as a wholetime professional writer?

As an alternative to going back to publishing, or to embarking on a completely new and strange career, fulltime writing had obvious attractions. I would be my own master. I could live where I liked. I could travel when and where I wanted to. Writing, again in theory, was what I enjoyed doing more than anything else. And now, thanks to my pre-war experience with Constable's, I ought by rights to know something about its commercial possibilities. I knew, or thought then that I knew, what sort of books sold, and what sort didn't. I would be hard-boiled; but I would never, of course, lower my standards. But there was a snag. I had complained all my working life that I never had enough time for writing. But with all the time in the world at my disposal, would I be able to think of anything to write about?

I remembered the disastrous holiday at Kitzbühel; and I remembered, too, an unfortunate episode when, about six months after I had written the "garden-mad" story, I had been staying by myself in a private hotel in Edinburgh. It was a dreary establishment, and I found the evenings lonely and boring. Obviously, I must occupy and amuse myself by writing a short story. In the event, I had been incapable of thinking of another plot. Evening after evening, hour after hour, I had sat in the beastly lounge of that beastly hotel with a pad of paper on my knee. The pad had remained blank, and I had once more endured headaches and a chronic sore throat. Would that happen to me if I adopted writing as a career? I did not fancy sitting morning after morning at my desk, vainly trying to think of something to write about, always with an aching head and a sore throat. That way lay despair and probably madness.

I played with the notion of trying to become quite a different kind of writer. I might, I thought, attempt to model myself on Harold Nicolson, whose books I greatly admired. I might try my hand at non-fiction, at reviewing, and at writing elegant, finished essays. But the only non-fiction book I had ever written had been a dreary manual which I had compiled while I had been on the staff of Chatham House; no literary editor, as far as I could see, would have any good reason for asking me to review books for him; and it was most unlikely that my essays, however elegant and however finished, would ever be accepted by anybody.

As dispassionately as I could, I reviewed my qualifications to be a wholetime professional writer. It was pretty certain that I was not a born novelist. I lacked the brand of mind that was always inventing stories about chance-met acquaintances, or even about people glimpsed in the street. The kind of mind that Phyllis Bottome possessed. In short, I lacked imagination. And I knew that I could no more write a novel that throbbed with passion, that was packed with memorable characters, or that moved at the pace of an express train, than I could fly. I might, conceivably, write a funny novel; but, as I correctly suspected, I also lacked the analytical, ice-cold approach of the true satirist. In short I was inhibited, unadventurous, uninventive, and unadaptably inflexible. Only genuine

59

scholars, people who had got fellowships at their Oxford colleges, wrote the kind of historical studies that I should have liked to have written. Only people far better read and far better qualified than myself could safely venture into the field of biography or literary criticism. If I had a talent at all, it was a tiny talent, a flickering flame that needed the most careful coaxing and cosseting. I like to think that I may have been very slightly under-rating my abilities; but there was a lot of truth in the conclusions that I reached.

One answer to my perplexing problem would have been to have given myself, say, a year in which to find out whether I could, or could not, make good as a writer. People who knew, deep down inside themselves, that they were born writers, or born painters, or born musicians, or born anything elses in the arts, traditionally chucked up everything, went to live in a cottage in the South of France on £1 a week, and emerged, after a period of ghastly privation and inner torment, as finished and successful practitioners. Or else they struggled along in an attic garret until at last the great day dawned, and success smiled. But such experimenters were genuinely convinced that they *were* born thises, thats, and the other things. I was by no means so certain. I also tended to dramatize the whole business —making it appear much harder than it really was. When I came out of the Army, my wife and I could quite well have gone off to the South of France or, for the matter of that, we could quite well have stayed at home, for a year; and we should have had between us a good deal more than £1 a week to live on. But I insisted on seeing all the difficulties and dangers. We both had highly critical families. Our nearest and dearest would almost certainly frown on an experiment of this kind. Scribbling was all very well, they would suggest, but surely it was a spare-time hobby? I was thirty-nine; and, after dithering about, I had apparently found a profession which I liked. Why did I not go back to it? I did not want anyone to be in a position to say "I told you so" if, after twelve abortive months, I had to confess that the experiment had failed, and that I now had no hopes of re-employment in Orange Street, or with any other publisher. And I secretly hankered, I admit, for the womb-like security of an office, for the routine of a settled, ordered, day-by-day employment, and for a cheque that came in at the end of each month. I fancied some regular employment; but not, I was convinced, as a publisher; and not, above all, with Constable & Company.

Looking back on it, this conviction seems rather strange; but certain things had happened which had been enough to daunt a far stronger and more resilient spirit than mine; and I recount them only because, as I now realize, they throw a certain amount of light on the other actors in the drama.

When, in September 1939, I had told Mr Kyllmann that I would be leaving to join the Army as soon as my call-up papers came through he had been, to all appearances, excited and delighted. Although he had been born and brought up in this country, the Chairman was of German extraction and, like many Britishers by adoption, he was a fanatical patriot. He was also a dyed-in-the-wool Manchester Liberal; and many of his dearest friends were German Jews. So he regarded the war in the light of a crusade; and he had tended to treat me, while I was waiting to become a soldier, as a knight who was preparing to buckle on his suit of shining armour. Indeed, in the first uneasy weeks of the war, I had seen more of him, and had worked more closely with him, than ever before. Michael Sadleir had stayed down in the country, no one had known what was going to happen, we had only a skeleton staff, and we had more or less run the firm between us. I had enjoyed myself enormously, doing all kinds of jobs that I had long wanted to do, but had never been allowed to. And in the course of several long heart-to-heart talks Mr Kyllmann had spoken of what we would do when, after the war, I became a director of the firm. He had appeared to regard this as a foregone conclusion.

While I was serving in the War Office, I had got into the habit of dropping in to see the Old Gentleman from time to time; and he had always been welcoming and, in his own queer way, almost affectionate. By this time I had grown distinctly fond of him. And when I was with 12 Corps I had heard, indirectly, of his astonishing courage. Though by no means young, and by no means—at least in his own estimation—robust, he had dutifully fire-watched night after night in Orange Street all through the blitz, and he had been on duty when Garland's Hotel, which adjoined the Orange Street premises, had been burnt to the ground. In addition to working very hard at running the firm, and helping to produce the *Nineteenth Century*—which was another love of his life—it had been clear that he had been seeing far more of the rough side of the war than I had.

Michael Sadleir I had hardly set eyes on; and when, later, I was sent on an Intelligence Course at Oxford, I had rung him up, knowing that he spent a good many week-ends with his father at Old Headington. I had thought it would be fun to see him again, to get first-hand news of Constable's, and to have a sight, perhaps, of old Sir Michael Sadler's remarkable collection of modern pictures. The immediate response to my suggestion that I might come up to Headington to luncheon on the following Saturday had been, I considered, a bit tepid. If I came *after* luncheon on Sunday, Michael had told me, he would be delighted to see me. I went; and we had sat in a dark little room, I had seen none of the pictures, and conversation had been distinctly stilted. I had told him that I was going on to tea in the nearby village of Beckley, and he had shown me a short cut across the fields, adding that he would walk some of the way with me. I had suggested that he should walk the whole way, and have tea with my brother-in-law and sister-in-law, whom I was sure he would like. I might, from his stricken expression of horror, have been suggesting that he should attend a hunt ball. But in the course of our short walk he had suddenly—and for the first time in our long acquaintance—opened up. He had told me that he had great plans for Constable's after the war;

and that I most definitely figured in them. We should publish fewer and better books—have a much more selective list. In 1938 and 1939 we had plunged into the choppy sea of "popular fiction." We had none of us much liked these novels, and they had not done well. All that nonsense could be forgotten, he had said; and he was seriously thinking of moving the firm, lock, stock and barrel, down to Headington. This had seemed to me an excellent idea. I loathed London, and I loved Oxford and Oxfordshire. We had parted, as I had thought, on the best possible terms.

A great silence had followed; and just before I left for the Far East, feeling insecure and longing for straws to clutch at, I had written to the Chairman inquiring how I actually stood if the war ever ended and if I ever got home again; and asking whether, in the event of a delay over demobilization, the firm would ask for my early release. Waiting for me in my tent in New Delhi I had found Mr Kyllmann's very odd reply. It was impossible at this time, he had written, to make any firm plans for the future—"and we regret that we can assume no responsibility whatever for our pre-war personnel." This statement had made me very angry. A knight, sweating under his shining armour in the Holy Land, would not, I thought, have enjoyed being classified as "pre-crusade personnel." I had sent off a rather stiff reply; and later, when I was at Headquarters, 14th Army, I had written to Michael Sadleir, reminding him of our talk on the way to Beckley. In due course I had received an answer so extraordinary that I had had to read his letter several times before I could take it in properly. "I have no recollection," he wrote, "of any conversation with you about Constable's future plans. Am I dreaming, or are you?" At this point I had given it up. Obviously, neither of them wanted me back and, even if they did, I should not want to go. And this feeling had been reinforced some weeks later when I got a letter from the Secretary of the Company telling me that the directors had decided that, as from the 1st of the following month, former members of the firm who were serving with the armed forces would receive, as a token of their esteem, a small monthly honorarium. As this had seemed to me—rather unfairly, as I now think—to be adding insult to injury, I had written begging to be allowed to decline the directors' offer; pointing out that His Majesty was kindly paying me about four times as much as I had ever received at Orange Street; and adding for good measure that this gesture would have been a good deal more acceptable if it had been made at the start of the war, when I had been a second-lieutenant.

None of the parties concerned ever referred again to this frustrating correspondence. At any time during the last sixteen years I could easily have sent for the relevant minute books of the Company and found out for myself what had occasioned these curious communications. I never did. I think I know what happened—or rather that I can make a shrewd guess. I imagine that each of them—the Old Gentleman and Michael—felt that, without consulting the other, he had committed himself to me too explicitly; that each, and this was completely in character, hated being committed; that I had forced the issue by my letters; and that each had, instinctively, withdrawn, expressing himself, in his alarmed timidity, more forcibly than he had intended. Of course there may have been some agreed plan for a post-war reorganization in which I had no place. This plan, like so many of their more ambitious projects, may have fallen through. But I doubt it.

As far as I was concerned, the mystery was deepened by the luncheon which I had with the Chairman very soon after I had returned for good from Ceylon at the beginning of August 1945. I never knew how Mr Kyllmann discovered that I had been repatriated. I had meant to keep the fact quiet until I had had a good think, and a good look round in other directions. But I received one of his curt notes asking me to lunch with him in the little restaurant in Soho which he frequented. Rather rashly I accepted. Always, before he went to the table that was reserved for him each day, the Old Gentleman repaired to a little windowless cubby-hole in which stocks of wine which might be needed in a hurry were kept. And it was in this holy of holies, jealously reserved for *habitués* of the place, that he told me that he and Michael were most anxious that I should return to Orange Street as soon as possible. I would be a full member of the Board, and I would be asked to invest only a modest amount of capital. I said that I would like more time to think it over.

After we had left the cubby-hole, and while we were eating our lunch, we became aware of excited chatter all round us, of early editions of the evening papers being handed round, and of people getting up and going over to talk to their friends at other tables. The Old Gentleman summoned one of the antique waiters, and asked him what was happening. The Americans, he was told, had dropped a giant bomb on Japan, and the war in the Far East was as good as over. With no inklings as to what the bomb was to mean, we drank a health to the men who had dropped it. For the last few months of my stint at Headquarters, SEAC, I had been bored to extinction by planning for a Press Ship which, in the coming reconquest of Malaya, was to carry all the accredited war correspondents and the public relations staff who looked after them. I had always prophesied that this ship would never sail out of Colombo Harbour. Evidently, for once in a way, I had been right.

Hedging, I told Mr Kyllmann, while we were drinking our coffee, that I would want to go on with my own writing. "Well," he said, "Michael writes, does he not, and that makes him a better rather than a worse publisher." I told him that I was not even sure that I wanted to go on being a publisher. This was an attitude of mind that he simply could not understand. Publishing—and Constable & Company—had been his whole life. It was still his whole life. I told him that if I did accept his generous offer I should never set the Thames on fire as a publisher. That the best I could offer him would be the conscientious services of —I hoped—a fairly trustworthy and reliable trace-horse. He said that publishers were made, not born. I doubted the truth of this statement then; and I still doubt it today. And then, as he lit his fourth cigarette after lunch, Mr Kyllmann began reminiscing—how, soon after he had joined the firm, he had bought the copyright of Nansen's *Farthest North* for what had then been considered a staggeringly large sum, and how, on publication day, Orange Street had been blocked by wholesalers' and booksellers' vans; how he had teamed up with Sir Frederick Macmillan, who had been his publishing idol, in the great Times Book Club battle; incidents in the long saga of Bernard Shaw's connection with the firm; and the story of the manuscript which had come in as one of a series of sociological studies—a worthy but singularly unexciting venture. The newcomer had been sent to the printers unread, proofs had been passed by the scholarly editor of the series, and no one in the office had as much as glanced at them. The book had been given a plain, type-set series jacket. It had subscribed as modestly as had been expected; and then, a week or so after publication, repeat orders had begun to pour in from bookshops in Green Street, and from other booksellers who specialized in sensational literature. They had tumbled to the fact that here was a detailed, and strictly factual, account of the white-slave traffic in South America. It was a Constable best-seller for years.

I had heard all these stories often enough before, but they served to bridge the gap between my pre-war and my brand-new post-war existences. And I could not help being flattered and pleased at being asked to come back to Orange Street. I have said that the Old Gentleman and Michael were timid. I had always been pretty timid myself about casting off into an unknown sea. Better the devil you knew . . .

But I suspect that it was curiosity, more than anything else, that led me, before we finally left the Escargot Restaurant on the afternoon that the atomic bomb was dropped on Hiroshima, to tell Mr Kyllmann that yes, I would be very happy indeed to accept the Board's generous offer. Curiosity to discover, from

66

the inside, how this intricate, tricky business was really conducted by this (to me) mysterious and unfathomable trio. Curiosity to know what each of the directors was really like. Curiosity to find out what their relations to one another really were. I had been on the outside, looking in. Now I had a chance of joining the charmed circle. I quite simply could not resist taking it.

Chapter Five

SO far as writing was concerned, after I had settled down
again into the old familiar routine of travelling up to London
five days a week on the 8.36, and coming home again on the
5.50, I made two false starts. Which was a pity, because either
of the books that I embarked on might, with a bit more knowledge, common sense and experience, have come off.

The first project was a novel. I had, before the war, written
three novels. The second, as I have already said, was rather worse
than the first. The third, on the whole, was the worst of all. But
the idea that I might be a novelist of sorts died hard; and up to
this point it had never seriously occurred to me to try my hand
at anything but fiction—to which category my three boys'
adventure stories and a pseudo-Buchanish thriller (best forgotten) had belonged. So now, despite the new light that was
supposed to have dawned, and despite the new understanding
that I was supposed to possess about the art and craft of writing
and the limitations of my own equipment as a writer, I blithely
tackled an idea for a novel that had occurred to me while I had
been reading, when I was serving with the 14th Army in Bengal,
everything I had been able to lay my hands on about Tibet.

As an idea it was not half bad. The priestly ruler of a small
remote Himalayan country that well might have been, but
wasn't, Tibet, has a vision when he is mortally ill that tells
him that his reincarnated self and successor will be born in an
English village; and he sends a trusted emissary to this country
in order, when the time comes, to locate the infant in question.
The emissary, on his arrival in London, is met by an old friend,

a land-owning retired Colonel in the Indian Army, who invites him down to stay in the country. Strange as it may seem, it is in the Colonel's own village that the destiny-fraught baby, after the ruler's death, is eventually discovered; but the object of the exercise was to portray the oddities of the ordinary round of everyday upper-class life in London and in the country as seen through the surprised eyes of a highly intelligent oriental who is visiting England for the first time. Far and away the best scene was the opening encounter between the Colonel and his guest at the Colonel's seldom visited London club. London clubs are easy meat for the social satirist, and social satire was what I was trying to achieve. I still maintain that it would strike an oriental as extremely odd that, in the washroom of a club, while it is considered unthinkable to put the towel on which one has just dried one's hands anywhere but straight into the dirty towel basket, to dispose in a similar fashion of the brushes with which one has just brushed one's hair would be held to be the act of a lunatic.

In favour of this light-hearted story was the fact that it *was* light-hearted; and that I was operating well within what ought to have been my capacity. I knew my London clubs and my retired Colonels inside out—I understood them, loved them with a kind of love-hate relationship, and was endlessly amused by them. I had lived in a small village all my life, so there was little I did not know about vicars, maiden ladies who did good works, impoverished people who lived in decaying country houses, financial magnates who lived in enormous country houses, and lady novelists who lived in olde worlde cottages and who believed, erroneously, that they understood their humbler neighbours. And I had finally deserted "passion" for the safer country of the foibles of everyday behaviour of perfectly ordinary people.

I doubt whether depicting even the simplest manifestations of passion had ever been my forte; and I was hamstrung, so far as venturing down the esoteric by-paths that many novelists find so handy, by the knowledge that, however many people failed to read my books when they came out, my mother, to whom I was devoted, would not be among them.

Family criticism, as it affects the output of writers, is a subject to which far too little attention has been paid; and I have sometimes wondered whether all the really outspoken novelists of my generation possessed either no mothers at all or mothers who were well versed in the shadier aspects of human behaviour. My mother wasn't; and I remember her telling me about an extraordinary visit she had had from a ridiculous woman who seemed to be in a great taking because her son, temporarily in charge of a youth club, had incurred considerable odium through giving one of his better-looking boys a brand new bicycle. "Unnecessary, I should have thought," my mother observed, "but extremely generous. I simply could not make out what all the fuss was about."

On a rather different level, I used to refrain deliberately from showing my wife anything I had written until it appeared in print. Some trenchant post-publication observations, however, suggested that she was a very shrewd critic; so I took to showing her first and second drafts. This has proved to be a painful but salutary procedure. A slow and apparently reluctant reader, instead of shutting herself up there and then in her room, disconnecting the telephone, and eagerly devouring every golden word I have written, she accepts a bundle of typescript with caution, and leaves it lying about, generally on the arm of one of the drawing-room chairs. Induced to turn her attention to the job on hand, she customarily reads a page or two, under the author's beady and anxious gaze, only to break off to do something much more important and pressing like writing a letter, or dead-heading the roses, or taking the dog out for a walk. At the end of about a week she delivers judgement. This bit, she says, is incomprehensible; and that bit excessively long-winded and boring. High words ensue, in the course of which I tell her that the passages in question caused me more mental anguish and effort to write than the whole of the rest of the book put together; and that if she had ever tried to write anything herself she would appreciate how unjust and unworthy such snap decisions must necessarily be. Then I go away, read through the bits she has condemned, and realize sadly how essentially right she is. Sometimes, on the other hand, she likes something that I have written; and that pleases me immeasurably.

Hands Across the Water was a near miss. It did quite well and got some good reviews, but it was a bit diffuse, the satire was a bit mild, and I would have done well to have revised it drastically. But I had failed to consult the critic on the hearth; and in any case, before it was finished I was panting to get started on my next book—my first venture in the realms of non-fiction.

I knew, or I thought that I knew, exactly what I wanted my next book to be. I wanted to write a book about the Hundred of Hoo. It would tell the story of this remote corner of the county of Kent from very early times right up to the present day; and it would tell it chiefly in terms of the people, great and small, who had lived in the Hundred down the years. It would also, I hoped, be a work of high literary merit—by which I probably meant a piece of writing of extreme and slightly precious literary elegance. I would do my best to bring the place as vividly alive as the people who had inhabited it. And, finally, the people and the events that I described would, if I could so contrive it, reflect the main stream of wider, national historical trends. It was an ambitious project. The Hundred of Hoo covers quite a small area; and I was asking rather a lot of it. My temperament, when it comes to planning books, has always been sanguine.

My ambition to write what might be described as a history book about the Hundred of Hoo stemmed from a number of different semi-choked springs of inspiration, some of them dating back to when I was a very small boy.

The Hundred of Hoo peninsula juts out between the mouths of the River Thames and the River Medway. On either side of a spine of high ground are the celebrated Thames and Medway marshes. In the Hundred, as it is always called locally, there are, in addition to the marshes, a handful of very small villages, and some first-class arable farming land. It is an out-by district, with its own idiosyncratic character—largely cut off both geographically and traditionally from the rest of the county.

Before the First World War my father rented a shoot on the Cooling marshes; and I can just remember him setting off from Meopham in a dog-cart with his gun and his Irish water spaniel, Maria. He was going, I was told, "to shoot down in the Hundred." I longed to be taken, but I never was. I cannot remember how I pictured the Hundred in my mind's eye, but I think I was convinced that it was an immensely wild and romantic place. There were two family stories connected with it that I never tired of hearing. One concerned Maria who, having retrieved faultlessly all day, suddenly, as evening was closing in, swam with a wild duck in her mouth to an islet in a creek and there, in full view of her enraged master, proceeded to devour the bird slowly and with evident enjoyment. The second concerned three small boys and their football. As he was starting to drive home one evening my father was stopped by a couple of urchins. "Hey, mister," one of the boys said, "our football's in the dyke." My father, who had had a long day and was anxious to get back and have his tea, suggested shortly that this was their concern rather than his. "Tommy's in there, too," the second boy volunteered as an afterthought. He was, too; and when my father fished him out he was pretty near his last gasp.

Then I read Dickens's *Great Expectations*, and I was told that the marshes that Dickens describes so well were these same Cooling marshes—"Ours was the marsh country, down by the river, within, as the river wound, twenty miles of the sea. . . . I found out for certain . . . that the flat dark wilderness beyond the churchyard, intersected with dykes and mounds and gates, with scattered cattle feeding on it, was the marshes; and that the low leaden line beyond was the river; and that the distant savage lair, from which the wind was rushing, was the sea." An enticing element of fear was now added to my idea of what the Hundred must be like.

But still I never went there. The kind of people who gave children's parties and who, later on in my life, organized children's tennis tournaments and boys' cricket matches, did not live in the Hundred. I only started going to the Hundred after I had been allowed to drive a car. Then, quite often, we used to go down to Grain to bathe. It was true that there was only a very narrow strip of sand, and if the tide was out it was necessary to splosh over what seemed like miles of oozy river mud before comparatively deep water was reached; but by this time I had become enchanted by the marshes themselves. And after we had dressed again among the rolls of disintegrating barbed wire left over from World War One, I used to insist on driving along the rutted track that led past Grain Fort to Port Victoria, a decayed, ghost-ridden place that had once aspired to being a cross-Channel port.

Then, one day in the autumn of 1940, I accompanied the Commander, 12 Corps, whose ADC I was, when he went to inspect the anti-invasion stop-line that had been dug along the bottom of Lodge Hill, close to Cooling village.

General Thorne had gained an impression—perhaps this had been my fault—that I knew the Hundred of Hoo like the back of my own hand. After all, it lay only about ten miles away from where I lived. Inevitably, the General insisted on climbing to the top of the hill. That done, we stood on the crest of the ridge looking north towards the Thames, where the sails of barges, showing above an invisible sea wall, produced an impression of ships sailing along on terra firma. At the foot of the hill was our car and our driver; and beyond them were the twin drum towers of Cooling Castle's gatehouse. Immediately to the east of the Castle was Cooling Church; and behind it was the flat stretch of the marsh, running back to the river. General Thorne, who had an engagingly inquisitive mind, wanted to know all about the Castle. Who had built it, and when, and for how long it had been a ruin. I had to admit, as we walked down the hill, that I did not know the answers to any of these questions. I had driven past the Castle dozens of times, but I had never bothered to discover anything about its history. I volunteered, and the General was unwise enough to take my word for it, that Cooling had been Pip's village, and the scene of the opening chapter in *Great Expectations*. I could show him, I said, the small lozenge-shaped tombstones in the churchyard. I felt ashamed that I knew so little about this marsh country for which I professed a deep affection. "As you are supposed to be an historian," the General remarked as we climbed back into the camouflaged Humber, "it might be a good idea if, one of these days, you wrote a history of this odd little corner of Kent."

I was an historian by courtesy only. It is true that I had read Modern History at Oxford; but after I had passed the preliminary examination at the end of my second term I had, for far too long, neglected to do any work at all. There had been so much else to do. Then, at the beginning of my third year, I had tumbled to the fact that unless I worked very hard indeed I should never get through my Schools. So I had worked like a black; but I had left it rather too late. Just occasionally, in the course of a hot sleepy summer's afternoon spent in the Codrington Library of All Souls reading Lord Clarendon's *History of the Rebellion* for my special subject, I had had a glimpse of how enticing the primrose by-paths of history could be; and then, day-dreaming over the old folio, I had promised myself that one of these days, my Schools safely over and a "first" in the bag, I would explore some of these paths for myself, and write a book about my findings. I pictured long fruitful days spent in the muniment room of some great country house in the Midlands; and evenings productively spent in my white panelled college room (I would have been given a fellowship) writing up my notes. I saw myself striding over the Oxfordshire countryside with John Buchan as my spiritual, if not my actual, companion—for his were the kind of literary-historical studies that I would like to write; his was the style, the magical touch, that I longed to emulate. Bar finding a suitable subject, pursuing it, and actually getting eighty thousand words or so down on to paper, the book that would astonish and delight the critics, and make my name as a popular historian, was as good as written.

It was these dreams, long forgotten in the disappointment of not getting a "first," that had fused, as we drove back to our headquarters at Tunbridge Wells, with my childish notions of the romance of the marsh country. When the war was over, I decided, I really would write a book about the Hundred of Hoo. When I was finishing *Hands Across the Water* the moment seemed to have arrived.

But before I could make a start on this ambitious project I had to collect a few facts. I was green at the job, in all conscience; but I realized that any historical study resembles an iceberg, inasmuch as the part that shows represents only about a quarter of the whole edifice. Though no one had ever been rash enough to devote a whole book to the Hundred of Hoo, it figured, generally rather incidentally, in a good many works of county and local history. I possessed, thanks to my historian grandfather, a reasonably good collection of Kent books; so I combed the volumes of *Archaeologia Cantiana* for Hoo references; I read, with mounting scepticism, Henry Smetham's accounts of the Hundred's villages in his *Rambles Round Churches*; and I entered into a long correspondence with the daughter of a one-time vicar of Allhallows, who had written an excellent account of his marsh-side village in a book called *The Story of an Outpost Parish*. I found that an ex-Sergeant-Major in the Royal Engineers had written a soldierly and informative pamphlet about the Isle of Grain, at the Hundred's eastern extremity. He had been stationed for a long time in Grain Fort. I haunted the invaluable London Library at lunchtime. I obtained innumerable books from the Kent County Library at Maidstone. I reread my old Oxford history notes; and rediscovered the virtues of Dr G. M. Trevelyan. Collecting facts, and making endless notes, is, to my way of thinking, by far the most entertaining part of writing a book of this kind. I am never happier than when I can sit in an armchair after dinner with a book on my knee, scribbling excerpts which, afterwards, I shall probably either lose or be unable to read.

At week-ends I used to go down to the Hundred as often as I could. Sometimes these excursions were successful, sometimes unsuccessful. I hated bothering people I did not know with questions; but I forced myself to do it. Clergymen, I considered, were fair game. The incumbents of these marsh-side villages ought, I reasoned, to know something of the histories of their parishes. After all, Mr Hammond had written a book about Allhallows. I was disappointed. The Hammond breed of clergyman had apparently died out. But I struck lucky in one or two other directions. I went to tea with a very old lady indeed, the daughter of James Pye, known locally as "The King of the Hundred," who had started farming operations at St Mary's Hoo in the year 1845. I discovered a retired farmer who had once been Master of the Hundred of Hoo Foxhounds, a short-lived enterprise. And the manager of the oil installation works at Grain was a pre-historian with a European reputation. John Evans must have regarded me and my inquiries as hopelessly amateur and frivolous, but he was endlessly helpful and kind.

The expeditions I enjoyed most were those which I undertook in order to collect material for my background scene-painting. I wished, time and again, that I could draw better. If I could have sat down and drawn selected bits of the Hundred of Hoo I should have got a far better idea of it; and then I should have been able to describe it more clearly and graphically. I did spend one whole morning lying in the rough grass on the edge of Northward Wood, which is now a bird sanctuary where herons nest in quite low scrub oaks, and where wild duck sit on their messy nests among the bluebells. The edge of Northward Wood commands an excellent view. At the bottom of a steeply tilted grass field is Decoy Farm, a nice old pink brick house with a roof splashed with orange lichen. Immediately behind the farm and its ilex trees and its buildings the marsh begins—a flat beige-coloured carpet shading into pale green, dotted with grazing sheep, its flatness broken, as Dickens had noticed, by an occasional gate, mound and raised causeway.

An overnight visit to the Hundred, when I unwisely took my wife with me, was less successful. I thought it would be a good idea to drive down one Saturday evening, spend the night in a pub, and then set off first thing on Sunday morning for a long walk, following the line of the sea wall. Impatient as ever, I chose a week-end far too early in the year. As we approached our pub—which had been rebuilt and modernized to attract such tourists as visited the Hundred in the summer—dusk, a very cold dusk indeed, was falling; and a north-east wind was whistling ominously across the Thames Estuary. My wife, who always declared that she found the marshes dreary, shivered and averted her eyes from the dismal scene. I tried to cheer her up by dilating on the cosy welcome that would be awaiting us. A keen student of John Buchan's historical novels, I am inclined to picture all inns as providing blazing fires, welcoming land-lords, and delicious steak and kidney pudding meals served with tankards of spiced, mulled ale. We were shown into a dank little sitting-room inefficiently heated by a smelly paraffin stove. When our supper came, it consisted of tinned soup, slices of Spam with bullet-hard tinned peas, and a trembling blanc-mange. It was as well that I had kept quiet about comfortable beds with sheets that smelled of lavender. Our bedroom, when we went upstairs, was even more discouraging than the sitting-room. It was a cave of draughts, the beds had lumps in them, and there were all too abundant traces of the room's previous occupant. He had evidently had fair hair which had been falling out in a distressing way; he had squeezed a great deal of toothpaste on to the sides of the only tooth glass; and he had apparently passed the time by cutting his toe nails—a proceeding which, on the evidence, must have been long overdue. We spent an unhappy and uncomfortable night in, as I tried to explain, a good cause.

Next morning I set out for my walk directly after breakfast. My wife said that she would come and meet me with the car. For a couple of miles I walked along the top of the sea wall, with sea lavender squashing under my feet at every step. It was low tide; and a great stretch of river ooze ran up to the earth-banked, stone-faced wall, the lower stones of which were green-stained and festooned with chocolate-brown seaweed. I soon got tired of this cheerless prospect, and struck inland across the marsh. From the top of Northward Hill the marsh had looked deceptively smooth and unbroken. In reality, as I found, it was cut up with dykes and fleets each with their screens of rushes, some small and reddish, others tall and bearded. In course of time I reached the dividing-line between the desert and the sown—Manor Way, a gated, grass-grown farm road, sheltered on the marsh side by a row of pollarded willows. On my left, as I walked along it, bonfires were sending up blue smoke that drifted across the steeply sloping arable fields and, as I walked towards my rendezvous with my car and my patiently waiting wife at Decoy Farm, I remember wondering how much, if at all, the scene had changed in the last three hundred years.

In connection with the Allhallows parish registers, which had been rescued from mouldering decay by the excellent Mr Hammond, I spent a long day at the office of the Diocesan Registry in Rochester. I found the crabbed handwritings of successive Allhallows churchwardens and overseers of the poor dauntingly difficult to read.

The Rochester Diocesan Registry was housed in the elegant

little Georgian house on College Green which is the place of business of the firm of solicitors of which first my grandfather, and then my father, had been the senior partner. Frequently, as I paused in my struggles with the squiggles in the vellum-covered records, and as I heard the Cathedral clock just outside chiming the quarters and the hours, I wondered if I had been a mug when I had failed to follow in the family's legal tradition. This would have been a nice peaceful office in which to have worked; and my grandfather, as I reflected, had thoroughly enjoyed his calling. He had lived in one of the big houses in the Precinct and, in addition to his many official appointments, he had had a large and flourishing private practice. An accomplished local historian in his spare time, he was a man whose deep learning and genuine scholarship were lightened and enlivened by an admirable if somewhat mordant sense of humour. He was fond of walking, gardening, buying and reading books, Egyptology, foreign travel, and looking at pictures; and every evening after dinner, when he was not playing whist at the Deanery or at one or other of the Canons' houses, he would work in his library until all hours, transcribing and annotating the deeds and terriers connected with the College of St Mary's at Cobham, where he had a country house; or adding to his voluminous notes on the *Textus Roffensis*, the principal treasure of the Rochester Chapter. If I had followed in his footsteps, I might have become as good and as conscientious a local historian as he had been.

My father, on the other hand, had not enjoyed working in the College Green office, and had urged me to adopt any other profession but the law. In the best Victorian tradition he had never seen eye to eye with my grandfather; and he always felt that he had been forced to join the family firm against his will. He was an excellent player of all games, and was devoted to hunting and to country pursuits generally. After he had married and had gone to live at my grandmother's house at Meopham, he used to ride in to Rochester each morning, putting up his horse in the Dean's stables. My grandfather and the elderly clerks, most of whom were Cathedral choristers, had been profoundly shocked that he should have interviewed his clients wearing riding breeches and leggings.

Before I went home, I gossiped with the then head of the firm, who recalled some of my father's later peccadilloes. When tarred roads had made riding in to Rochester a pain rather than a pleasure, he had taken for a time to travelling by train. But that had bored him. Unable to drive a car himself, he had one day bought a motor-bicycle. After a minimum of instruction he had set off gaily one spring morning for the office. He had reached his destination—heaven alone knows how; but when he had tried to mount his machine for the return journey —it was necessary to run alongside it and then jump on—the brute had fairly run away with him, and together they had charged a flower-seller's barrow, collapsing in a heap of tumbled daffodils. My father's reactions to this mishap had been entirely in character. Disembarrassing himself and his machine from the flowers, and having curtly informed the irate barrow-owner that he had no right to peddle his wares in the Precinct, he had remounted his devilish contraption and had swept fearlessly into the traffic of the High Street. My father never lacked courage.

*　　　*　　　*

I was lucky in the crop of people and events that the Hundred produced.

There was Sir John de Cobham, the third baron Cobham, who built Cooling Castle—one of the very last fully defensive castles to be put up in this country—in the year 1381. He had been badly frightened by the Peasants' Revolt, and was taking no chances. There was Sir John Oldcastle, Lord Cobham, who married the third baron's granddaughter and heiress. His nickname was the "Lollardus Lollardorum"; Foxe described him as "the Blessed Martyr of Christ, the Good Lord Cobham"; and on Christmas Day, 1417, he was hanged, and burnt hanging, in St Giles's Fields. There was the seventh baron Cobham who played an extremely tricky rôle in Wyatt's Rebellion. For reasons far too long to go into here, I came to the conclusion that he had invited his nephew, Thomas Wyatt the Younger, to knock Cooling Castle down on 29 January 1554. There were the churchwardens and overseers of the poor of Allhallows, about whom I managed in the end to discover a good deal. There was Dr Peter Gunning, Bishop of Ely, a native of the Hundred, who may or may not have taken refuge in the Cockham woods when the Royalists were after him. There was Thomas Aveling, who invented steam-rollers; Henry Pye, who revolutionized farming practice and drained the Hundred's marshes; and there was Sir Edward Watkin, chairman of the South-Eastern Railway Company, who had the wild idea of establishing a cross-Channel port at the Hundred's eastern extremity. And finally there was my favourite character of all— the Rev. Robert Gascoyne Burt.

Mr Burt was born in the year 1791, and he held the living of St Mary's Hoo, the Hundred's smallest village, for fifty-nine years; and the adjacent living of High Halstow for fifty-one years. He also owned a house in Twickenham, in which he lived for three months out of every twelve. His life was an exceptionally quiet one. He was accustomed to hold a morning service at St Mary's and at High Halstow on alternate Sundays. During his annual absences at Twickenham, services in both churches were allowed to lapse. He is said never to have composed a sermon; and he very seldom delivered one. At St Mary's, the men sat on one side of the nave and the women on the other. The children were herded into a pew in the chancel, where they were supervised by a tyrant called Collins, who maintained order with the help of a stout stick. The parish clerk, Justice by name, frequently dropped off to sleep, waking up to intone "Amen" at inappropriate moments. Music was at first supplied by a local band, but as it also played in other churches, St Mary's only benefited from its presence every fourth Sunday. Later, a barrel-organ that played six hymn tunes was purchased by the rector. Church collections were spasmodic. When Mr Burt decided that it was time to have one, he stationed himself at the church door after the service armed with a dinner-plate which he had tactfully primed in advance with a sovereign and a penny. No one could then feel that he was giving either too much or too little. The rector's private life was equally unsensational. He married, but had no children. Except when he was taking church services, he eschewed clerical dress. Each year, on a stated day, a new top hat was despatched to him from an eminent hatter's in St James's Street. He kept a carriage and a pair of grey horses, and on fine afternoons he would drive out along the narrow bumpy lanes of the Hundred in this inappropriately grand conveyance. It delighted me to reflect that the private means that allowed this retiring clergyman to lead his sheltered existence derived from half an hour's shady work put in on 21 December 1785. Mr Burt's father, the Rev. Robert Burt, had been the "unnamed" clergyman who was heavily bribed to marry Mrs Fitzherbert to the Prince of Wales. There is a tablet to his memory on the wall of St Mary's Church.

It is sad to have to admit that *The Hundred of Hoo*, when it was published, was something of a failure. For this I had no one to blame but myself. Partly because I was impatient to get it finished, and partly because I had signally failed to apply the lessons which I was supposed to have learnt about writing, I took far too little trouble about the book's composition. *Hoo* was not only poorly constructed, flippant in tone and carelessly written, it also contained anything and everything about the Hundred of Hoo that I had managed to discover. If ever a book displayed an author's failure to select and discriminate, that book was *The Hundred of Hoo*. Each discovery I had made, however trivial or irrelevant, had appeared to me, at the time, to be a small triumph; and it had seemed a pity not to share all these small triumphs with my readers.

The reviewers, when the time came, instead of hailing it as the local history book to end all local history books, were, in some instances, justifiably severe in their criticisms. The *Spectator* asked Miss Victoria Sackville-West to review it. I already admired her books, and I later came to admire and like her quite enormously as a person. It was a bitter blow when she observed that while I seemed to know a great deal about the Hundred of Hoo, it was a pity that I was apparently incapable of writing straightforward and grammatical English. For weeks, on the principle, I suppose, of a hair shirt, I kept this press-cutting in my wallet, sadly bringing it out from time to time to read. And for long enough I was unable to face going to lunch at the club, fearing that everyone there must be aware of my recent, well-deserved, and (as I believed) horribly public humiliation.

Chapter Six

WHILE I was wrestling with *The Hundred of Hoo* at week-ends, I was working pretty hard, week in, week out, at Orange Street. I should like to think that when I had gone back to Constable's at the end of the war I had known exactly what I was doing, and that I had been able to contemplate the career that presumably stretched before me with clear, unclouded eyes. To say that, up to a point, I had known what I was letting myself in for would have been nearer the mark.

My pre-war apprenticeship had certainly convinced me that my original romanticized dream or vision of what being a publisher was like was mostly moonshine. There was more to it, I had realized, than sitting at an enormous desk in an enormous room proffering tea, toasted buns and good advice to young writers; staying with successful authors in the South of France; and reading manuscripts and spotting potential best-sellers on Saturdays. Books, I had discovered, once they had been accepted for publication, had to be printed and bound—which was a costly business; and then they had to be promoted and sold—which necessitated the expenditure of more money and the employment of quite a large staff. Somehow, money had to be found to pay the weekly wages bill, the directors' fees each month, authors' royalties twice a year, and the multitude of overhead expenses that any business incurs. And every penny had to come from the sales of new books and backlist titles. Proceeds from subsidiary rights—sales to paperback houses, sales of serial rights, and so on—were not then considered nearly as important as they are today.

By no means every new book, I knew, made a profit. A good many did not even get their money back. The sale of a steady backlist title was apt suddenly to stop. It had been borne in on me that, viewed dispassionately, general publishing was, quite possibly, a mug's game. Take book advertising. We had spent, as I had observed, several thousands of pounds every year advertising our new books in the Sunday papers and in the weeklies. The object, presumably, had been to bring these new publications, and any favourable comments they might have elicited from reviewers, to the attention of the reading and book-buying public. But plenty of people who should have known what they were talking about had assured me that the only book advertising that in fact made a ha'porth of difference to sales was the advertising of books that were already selling. Advertising could increase the volume of sales; it could not set the ball rolling. It was possible to spend hundreds or thousands of pounds boosting a slow seller or a complete non-starter, and it would be money down the drain. And yet, week by week, we had advertised every new book we had brought out. Why? Because, as it had been explained to me, we could not afford not to. As a start, the real object of the exercise was not, necessarily, to advertise this title or that, but to advertise the imprint. If Constable's stopped advertising except when they had a big-selling book on their hands, or drastically curtailed the amount that they spent on advertising, their rivals in the trade, their customers, and everyone else in the small publishing world would assume that the firm was on the brink of dissolution; and we should no longer be able to obtain credit from printers, binders, and paper-makers. Secondly, authors expected their books to be advertised. I could appreciate that. As each new book of mine had come out, I had looked for advertisements almost as eagerly as I had looked for reviews. How could people hear about this masterpiece, read it, like it, and recommend it to their friends if it was not properly and, if possible, lavishly advertised? Publishers, and especially my own publishers, I had felt, simply did not know their job; and no anti-advertising argument, which I was prepared to accept as a publisher, could convince me as an author. Thirdly, if a publishing house did not advertise, or only advertised when they had something to shout about, literary agents would offer their best manuscripts elsewhere, established authors would become restless, and new writers would submit their books to more lavishly-spending firms. Three perfectly good arguments for doing something that, *per se*, was economically indefensible. Publishing, I had discovered, was full of anomalies like that. It entailed a vast amount of careful, detailed, skilled and sometimes fiddling work all down the line; and the risking of considerable capital sums for, at the best, rather small returns.

I had known all too well why people went into publishing. I had also gained an insight into why, once they had become publishers, they remained publishers. Publishing, I had decided, had to be regarded primarily as a business. But general publishing (as opposed to specialized publishing—school text-books, law books, medical, scientific and technical books) was also a game, played according to rules, and decided by skill, strength, or luck. And just as natural ball-game players, in order to be happy, had to play cricket or football or golf or squash, so natural publishers had to publish. Whether I was, or was not, a natural publisher was something I had yet to find out.

As soon as I was back in Orange Street I did my best to keep the promise I had made to the Chairman when I had lunched with him at the Escargot Restaurant. I embarked on my activities as a trace-horse. In my apprentice days I had longed to try my hand at this, that and the other job; and I had never been given the chance. Now I discovered that my fellow-directors were only too anxious to off-load work on to me; and I accepted this situation with gratitude and satisfaction.

The firm, I found, was far better off financially than it had been when I had left it in 1939. The destruction of enormous numbers of bound books and of unbound sheets by enemy bombing during the war, an unprecedented demand for reading matter (it had not much mattered what) by bored people in the armed forces and by equally bored civilians, indiscriminate mass book buying by service agencies, and a dearth of paper for new books, had meant that stocks of old books which, pre-war, had been written off as worthless, had sold like hot cakes. Soon after war had broken out Constable's had published Michael's novel, *Fanny by Gaslight*, and keeping *Fanny* in print had been a most profitable way of using a fairly high proportion of our meagre paper ration. By 1945 some pretty large accumulated debts had been paid off; and the outlook for the future should have been rosy. On the other hand, to keep in the race, we were faced with reprinting most of our standard backlist titles, stocks of which were either dangerously low or non-existent; these reprints would compete with new books for such paper as we could extract from the Paper Controller; production costs had risen steeply, and were continuing to rise; and neither we nor any of our friends and rivals were prepared to face the hurdle of increasing the published prices of our books proportionately. Things were not going to be as easy as they promised. They seldom are in publishing.

Step by step I took over from O.K. (as I now called Mr Kyllmann) the general supervision of the production department and all its works, the supervision of the trade department and all its ramifications, and the conduct of our running battle with the Paper Control at Reading. In time I took over from Michael the handling of American rights, which meant selling, or trying to sell, our non-agented books to American publishing houses. And from Martha Smith, again in course of time, I took over advertising, the compiling of our seasonal lists, and that awful old bugbear, the General Catalogue.

O.K. continued to supervise the firm's finances, and to cope with Bernard Shaw and with most of his old pre-war authors. Any new authors who came his way he passed on to me. Michael was the chief book-getter, the editor-in-chief (though "editor" was not a term we ever used), and the chief author-handler; and Martha joined forces with him, removing herself from the glassed-in lookout post that she had occupied in the general office, and establishing her desk and her filing cabinets in Michael's room. She became, in effect, a kind of super private secretary or personal assistant. It was an arrangement that worked admirably. Michael needed company, support and, at times, stiffening. Martha supplied these elements. Sometimes I found them a formidable combination. Two against one, with age and experience and prestige on their side, was, I used to think, hardly fair. I began to collect some new books and some new authors of my own.

Generally, I suspect, in any publishing house there can be seen in operation what might be termed the natural law of publishing succession. For a time the stars revolve in their orbit in due and proper order. The "senior star," less brilliant perhaps than it once was, holds its own. It is still the chief adornment of this particular little firmament. Next to it, the "up and coming star" is increasing in brightness all the time, but has not yet outshone its senior. Then, well down the scale, comes the "junior star," slowly growing brighter, but remaining nevertheless, comparatively unobtrusive. At last a moment arrives when this equilibrium is suddenly shattered. The "senior star" begins, unmistakably, to wane. The "up and coming star" is seen to be at its zenith. The "junior star" is abruptly in the ascendant.

It was evident to me, after I had been back at Constable's for only a short time, that O.K. was now a waning star. Throughout the war he had borne much of the heat and burden of the day at Orange Street. Though he had enjoyed it all enormously, it had taken a lot out of him. He was an old and tired man. But he was still a force to be reckoned with. The Achilles heel of many highly skilled publishers is their conviction that they are also highly skilled financiers. O.K., first-rate publisher as he unquestionably was, suffered from this dangerous delusion. He appeared to be guided in his financial policy by two manias.

The first was the maintenance of the firm's balance at the Bank at as high a figure as possible. This meant that he authorized the payment of outstanding accounts as seldom as possible and, whenever he could manage it, he persuaded Constable's creditors to accept bills. The second was a passion for extracting discounts. His favourite printers were MacLehose, of Glasgow. He favoured them partly because they were very good printers, and partly because their directors were so nice. But he ordained that they should be given a lot of our printing largely because he had persuaded them to give us a 10 per cent. discount. MacLehose made no secret of the fact that they merely added this 10 per cent. to their composition and printing charges. Everyone in the house, including O.K. himself, was aware of this. It did not matter. The magic words "Less 10 per cent." appeared at the foot of every MacLehose invoice; and he was happy. He had got the better of a shrewd Scottish Board.

O.K.'s dealings with Bernard Shaw were devious, complicated and, so far as the rest of us were concerned, largely wrapped in mystery. From the start of his connection with Constable's, as far back as the beginning of the century, Shaw had insisted that his books should be published on a commission basis. That is to say, instead of the publishers bearing all the costs of production, and pocketing the proceeds from sales less, in due course, the author's royalty, Shaw himself paid for the printing and binding of his books, bought the paper that they consumed, and himself pocketed the proceeds from their sale, less a fixed commission which Constable's deducted. He was, he considered, being sharp and clever—most authors were such fools when it came to business. I once read quickly through the Shaw-Constable correspondence, covering a long span of years. Several things emerged quite clearly from these bundles of old letters. From start to finish, Shaw had an abiding faith in O.K. as a publisher, and in Constable's ability to handle the sale of his books efficiently. By that, I do not mean to suggest that he always took O.K.'s advice on publishing questions; or that he never criticized Constable's methods. His letters were full of accusations, exhortations, instructions, expostulations, and condemnations; and he took O.K.'s advice remarkably seldom. But he always (until very nearly the end) consulted him; and he stayed with the firm to the finish.

As Shaw paid for his print and his paper and his binding, he did the ordering and the approving himself. He had strong views on typography, and on what a book ought to look like. So had O.K.; and their views seldom coincided. Again, as he was paying the piper, Shaw called the tune in such matters, for example, as the first printing numbers for his books. This was also a subject on which O.K. considered himself, with justification, an expert. There were frequent clashes. But the significant thing is that Shaw always, or very nearly always, asked O.K. for his opinion. He could recognize an expert when he saw one. It was seldom advisable, he evidently felt, to follow the expert's advice—experts were so often wrong. But it was wise to hear what they had to say. He was a shrewd old bird; and in O.K. he recognized another shrewd old bird.

On one issue Shaw was absolutely adamant. Throughout their long association O.K. never stopped trying to persuade his most important author that commission publishing was unsatisfactory; and that he would do far better if Constable's shouldered all the risks, and if he was paid a royalty like everyone else. Shaw rightly suspected that Constable's would do far better under such an arrangement; and he stuck his toes in and would not budge. Now and then, when O.K. suggested some special project—a limited collected edition, or an illustrated edition of a single volume—G.B.S. might relent. He relented, I suspect, only when he was doubtful whether the project in question would pay off.

Where O.K. and Shaw came into head-on collision was over money. There had never been, as O.K. used often and proudly to tell me, any formal agreement between Constable & Company and George Bernard Shaw. "Simply, my dear Arnold, a few scribbled lines on a half sheet of writing paper." What O.K. did not tell me was that there had, in fact, been a number of agreements entered into from time to time whereby Constable's pledged themselves to pay Shaw the money that was due to him at stated and prescribed intervals. The money that came in from the sale of Shaw books, less Constable's commission, belonged to Shaw. That was an incontrovertible fact. But this money was paid in to Constable's, not to Shaw; and this gave O.K. his chance to hoard. Sometimes, Constable's must really have needed the thousands of pounds that in no sense belonged to the firm. More often, I suspect, O.K. could not bear to part with these large sums, simply because they made the firm's bank balance look so imposing. Shaw stormed, raved, threatened, and cajoled. How, he demanded, could he pay his printers' bills, his binders' bills, and his paper-makers' bills when Constable's hung on to cash that was rightly his? And what about those firm promises about payments that had been made last year, and the year before? He was bankrupt, starving, down and out. He did not, literally, know where to turn for his next meal. O.K. would write brief, bleak letters suggesting payments of £500 a time, spaced out over the next twelve months. Shaw would be pacified; there would be peace for a time; and then it would all start up again.

I was amazed, reading these letters, by Shaw's tolerance, patience and good humour. He hardly ever wrote a nasty letter; and his most violent expostulations and remonstrances were, as a rule, basically good-tempered. He had the lightest of of light touches as a correspondent, and a lot of his letters were extremely entertaining. I imagine for one thing that he never really needed the money. For another he must have been confident that it would be forthcoming in the end. And he was obviously very fond of O.K. This affection was reciprocated, though I always gained the impression that O.K. was secretly terrified of Shaw. But he hero-worshipped him; and Shaw probably liked that. Shaw, I am sure, had summed O.K.

up. He recognized his qualities and his failings. For O.K., Shaw was the most resplendent feather in Constable's cap.

When I rejoined Constable's, Shaw and O.K. were both old men. Whatever failings anyone has when he is young and middle-aged, it is certain that these failings will be accentuated when he grows old. Shaw in his eighties and nineties came genuinely to believe that he stood on the brink of financial ruin. O.K. clung to the Shaw money as it came in with an even fiercer determination. And there were plenty of problems looming ahead. Goodness knows how many Shaw sheets had been destroyed when Leighton Straker's binding works had been bombed. Characteristically, Shaw's reaction to this news had been to write to O.K. saying that, as disposers of his books, German airmen had Constable's beaten to a frazzle. There would have to be a big reprinting programme; and G.B.S. was still writing plays. In his prime, Shaw had been, on the whole, realistic and sensible about printing numbers, and about the other publishing decisions he had had to take. Shaw in his eighties and nineties was apt to be perversely silly, vastly over-estimating the demand for his later work. He became less and less willing to take O.K.'s advice; and on one occasion he deeply wounded the Old Gentleman's pride by suddenly informing him that he had arranged with Penguin Books to issue paperback editions of a number of his works. O.K. belonged to the generation of publishers who profoundly disapproved of allowing paperback houses to handle "their" titles. That Shaw should have conducted these negotiations behind his back—though he had, of course, every right to do so—seemed to O.K. a monstrous insult; and he could do nothing about it. Thereafter their relations were never again as cordial as they once had been.

Michael, Martha and I were allowed to know very little of what was going on in the Shaw department. An iron curtain had long ago been lowered, and remained in place until, late in the day, I was invited to squeeze myself behind it. Michael was generally pleased to assume that Shaw was a crashing bore.

92

Martha complained, and with good reason, that the firm did not make nearly enough money out of the Shaw connection.

For the rest, O.K. pottered along. Each year the tale of his authors dwindled. He had his faithful Mr Bates, who, as his secretarial duties were reduced to perhaps a couple of letters a day, took on other duties, though he was constantly interrupted in them by the ringing of the Chairman's bell—and woe betide him if he did not answer its summons in double quick time. As often as not, he would be instructed to remove one completely unimportant paper from the Chairman's out-tray. I was another victim of the Old Gentleman's enforced, or self-enforced, idleness. He was always ringing through to me to ask whether I could spare him a minute or two. I would be waved to the leather-covered armchair, offered the inevitable cigarette from the same old tin box, my health would be inquired about, and I would be subjected to a lecture, reminiscence, or an exposition on the international situation. Then O.K. suffered another blow. First, the *Ninteeenth Century* acquired a new editor with whom he did not altogether see eye to eye; and then its proprietors decided to set up their own office organization. His empire was crumbling.

Michael had certainly not come through the war unscathed. His elder son had been killed, a blow from which I believe he never really recovered. But in a material sense he emerged from it with a greatly enhanced prestige. He was now recognized not only as a distinguished and graceful writer, but as a best-selling novelist; and he was an accepted authority in so many fields—book collecting, bibliography, Victorian fiction, nineteenth-century London. He must, surely, have been one of the shyest, least assertive, least well-known literary celebrities of all time. So far as his publishing activities went, he was almost certainly, when I returned to Orange Street, at his zenith. But his attitude remained unchanged. He was as meticulously considerate of other people's opinions at manuscript meetings as he had ever been; and I found that he had one rare and outstanding virtue

93

as a colleague. He was always prepared, when occasion arose, to give a firm decision on any point at issue—but if I felt later that, for some reason, this decision was wrong, and if I went and told him so, he would be perfectly prepared to reopen the question, hear what I had to say and, if I could persuade him that I was talking sense, abandon his previous position with complete good humour. Very few men of his eminence would have behaved as Michael behaved. But occasionally I fancied that he might be growing tired of publishing. At some time between the ages of fifty and sixty most publishers, I suspect, lose some of their zest for the publishing game. They are inclined, then, to look back and to think that publishing ten or fifteen or twenty years ago was more fun. They do not altogether like the way that publishing is going—new trends, new ideas, new faces, and a new code of manners. Things, they feel, are not what they used to be. The new books that are doing well are not always the kind of books they like. Michael may have been feeling all these things—I think he probably was; but his keenness and thoroughness never slackened, and some of his most notable publishing triumphs were still to come.

As a person, I never began to know him really well. Sometimes I felt that I understood him, progressively, less and less. He was not easy to know. After I had joined the Board, he used, now and then, to ask me to dine with him. We always dined *à deux* in a restaurant, returning afterwards to the book-lined sitting-room in his London flat. Invariably, on such occasions, I either found myself tongue-tied or, through shyness, I talked too much. He, I fancy, found himself in much the same case. I gained the impression, though I may well have been wrong, that he was mildly unhappy; that he felt that he was not making the fullest use of his remarkable talents. He had a tremendous, hero-worshipping admiration for his father, against whose achievements he measured his own attainments. His own attainments seemed to me to be considerable enough. I may have been seeing a reflection of my own perplexities in another

94

man's mind, but I used to wonder whether he was torn between going on as a publisher or devoting all his time to writing. I suspected that, while in his heart of hearts he would have liked to have been free to write, he was less certain of himself as a writer than as a publisher; that the routine of the office soothed his nerves; that he dreaded the loneliness of a writer's life; and, strange as this may seem in a man with so many interests, that he feared he might be bored. So he remained very much a fulltime publisher, and a reasonably prolific author. I could not imagine then, and I cannot imagine now, how he got through all the work that he accomplished, and how he contrived to do it as well and as thoroughly as he did. It must have been a most frightful strain; and in the end the strain told.

Of all the people I have ever encountered, Michael was one of the most fascinating and one of the most baffling. On the surface, he appeared to be a mass of contradictions. He could be fantastically generous; and chillingly the reverse. He could be heart-warmingly encouraging; and he could administer douches of the coldest of cold water. He could be understanding one day; and coldly remote the next. A very sensitive man himself, he was often curiously insensitive in his dealings with other people. He would write a wounding letter to an author, or say something unkind to a member of the staff, without, apparently, having an inkling of the almost inevitable effect. He was genuinely surprised when people were angry or hurt. I was at once too old to be his faithful disciple—a rôle that I would have gladly filled if he had ever given me the chance; and not old enough to be an intimate friend. And, temperamentally, we appeared to be poles apart. He was an unrepentant romantic, and he probably regarded me as a *terre-à-terre* realist. He liked to picture himself as a convinced rebel against all conventions; rightly, he must have regarded me as hopelessly conventional. He may have thought me an unredeemable prig—though greedy, I was never much of a drinker, and I found the seamy side of London life, whether in the nineteenth or the twentieth century, sordid and dreary rather than exciting. He was adventurous, and I was unadventurous. He thought that many of my interests and enthusiasms were stodgy. These differences, which were probably more apparent than real, formed a barrier which, until near the end of his life, tended to keep us at arms' length. It was partly my fault. I had begun by being frightened of him—but in those days I was secretly frightened of most people; and my lack of self-confidence probably made me appear arrogant. I wish he could have known how much I admired him and envied his talents, and how grateful I should have been for his helping hand with my own writing. But, underneath, he was a consistent person—a much more straightforward person, I suspect, than he appeared to be. As a colleague he could not have been nicer, more conscientious, more generous, or more understanding. And he had the inestimable gift of an excellent and reliable sense of humour. If I could make him laugh, a battle was half won.

The war had had a softening effect on both Michael and Martha. Everyone in the house noticed it, and remarked on it. Michael was gentler, kinder, and more approachable. Martha was much mellower. And, so far as the ups and downs of publishing fortune were concerned, Constable's enjoyed a comparatively halcyon period.

Looking back on the books with which he was intimately involved during any given period, I suppose that any publisher will immediately think of notable successes and of resounding failures; of best-sellers, and of horrors that either got critical slatings or involved his firm in expensive libel actions. He will also recall—I certainly do—plenty of good books that were neither successes nor failures, but came somewhere in between.

Of course, from this time, I remember Harold Nicolson's *King George V*, which must have been so hideously difficult to write, and which was so outstandingly well written. O.K. was prouder of it, I think, than of any other book we published while I was at Orange Street. Like all Harold Nicolson's books it "went through" with the greatest possible ease—but then he was, and is, a publisher's dream author. His output was steady and regular, he never fussed, he was never difficult, he was ridiculously grateful for anything that anyone in the firm did for him, and his books always sold. Months in advance he would name the precise day when he expected to finish whatever he was currently working on, and on that day, without fail, a beautifully typed manuscript would be delivered, complete down to the last comma, and accompanied by all the requisite material for the illustrations, meticulously captioned. Rumour has it, though this is something that I have never checked, that he customarily devotes great pains to ensuring that all the chapters in each of his books should contain precisely the same number of words.

And of course I remember David Cecil's *Lord M*, Mrs Woodham-Smith's *Florence Nightingale*, and Rawicz's *The Long Walk*.

David Cecil, from one point of view and from one point of view only, was not altogether a publisher's dream. Although he was chary of ever saying when anything he was writing was likely to be finished, it was prudent to add at least six months to any estimate that might, in the end, be forthcoming; and he had a habit of correcting his proofs with a blunt pencil when in transit between Oxford and London in an apparently violently vibrating railway carriage. But, apart from these inconsiderable drawbacks, he is not only the nicest possible person with whom a publisher could ever hope to have to deal; he is also, in my estimation, one of the few twentieth-century writers, so far, who will still be read with intense pleasure in a hundred years' time.

Mrs Woodham-Smith's first book came to us because Michael had planned a series of Victorian biographies. Not all the titles in this series were so triumphantly successful. *The Long Walk* we owed to Richard Sadler's persistence in following up a clue—a chance remark made to a newspaperman in a London public house. The book that resulted was one of those rare collaborations between a man with an extraordinary story to tell, and a first-class writer who never once obtruded his own personality or his own views.

In the course of nature, at this as at any other time, we had our troubles; and the one I remember best was a narrow escape from disaster. We had accepted a first novel; and I had asked its young author whether his hero—a foreign gardener employed by a retired British general—was drawn even remotely from real life. If this had been the case, we could not have touched the book with a barge pole. He assured me categorically that the gardener and all the other characters were his own brain-children—that there had never been, as far as he knew, any such people. When this novel had reached the proof stage I happened to stay a week-end with one of my brothers-in-law; and at dinner on Saturday night he mentioned a neighbour, with whom he had once served in India, who had had some trouble with a foreign gardener. The story as he related it sounded ominously familiar, and so did the rest of the people involved. Tackled when I got back to London, the author blithely admitted that every character in his book had in fact been taken straight from life.

I had been curious to discover how O.K., Michael and Martha Smith worked together, and how they contrived to run the business. Now I had my chance to find out. For all practical purposes it was, I found, a tug-of-war, with Michael and Martha on one end of the rope, and O.K. on the other. This suggests a prolonged tussle—and in a sense that is what it amounted to. However civilized a publishing firm may be, there is, going on all the time, consciously or unconsciously, a struggle for mastery. The law of the herd is also the law of the publishing house. O.K. was the old bull; and unlike many chairmen who are past their primes he did not have the advantage that comes from holding a majority of the shares. But in another sense it was a very polite contest. O.K. was genuinely devoted to Michael, and had an enormous, ungrudging and completely unselfish and unjealous admiration for his talents. Michael, in his turn, was very fond of O.K.—the situation would have been impossible if this had not been the case. Indeed, it was hard not to be fond of the Old Gentleman, maddening as he very often was. But O.K. clung to the control he had exercised for so long. His day had passed, his triumphs were old history, and yet he would not relinquish his hold.

Michael and Martha held all the cards; I realized that they were almost certainly in the right; and yet I sometimes used to feel very sorry for the Old Gentleman. He had many endearing traits. In a lot of ways—his enthusiasm for new Constable books, for example—he remained surprisingly young in heart. He was very easily hurt. And, as a publisher, he was essentially wise. "Always remember," he once told me, "that authors are queer folk. If they weren't queer folk, they would not write books." "Always listen carefully to what your travellers have to say," he would often observe, "and then do the opposite." In the nicest possible way he was a snob. Not a social snob, but an intellectual snob—and in particular what would now be termed an Establishment snob. He simply could not resist an eminent politician, an eminent diplomat, or an eminent editor. Talking to them made him feel that he was "in the know"—and he loved being in the know. *Who's Who*, which he was always consulting, was his stand-by. Sometimes one of the objects of his profound admiration would come to Orange Street and, instead of going to his office, would go instead to see Michael. O.K. would discover this treachery, and then he would be deeply hurt, even after Michael afterwards complained that the fellow had wasted his time and had bored him stiff. It did not matter. The Old Gentleman's feelings had been wounded. He could be endlessly tiresome, wasting everyone's time, and for ever ringing bells and ordering some inappropriate person to rush out into the rain and get him a taxi. And then, as often as not, he would walk off without waiting for the taxi to arrive.

He used to tell me again and again that his dearest wish was that he might die at his desk in his office. I argued that this was a selfish ambition, that it would be a great inconvenience and embarrassment to all of us, and that it would be much better if he could arrange to die in his bed in his own house. He held strong views about most things, and he was often right; but he could be argumentative, glum, and deliberately wrong-headed. I sat through some very painful meetings when the Old Gentleman's hands trembled uncontrollably, when his brown eyes filled with tears of frustration, and when, unable to bear it any longer, he stumbled shakily out of the Boardroom. Sometimes my sympathies were with him; sometimes, I am afraid, with the other side. But O.K.'s outstanding virtue, which we all recognized, was his genuine love of books. That, and his abiding passion for Constable's. Not all publishers really love books.

The methods of conducting the business of the firm on the directors' level were, I found, a curious mixture of formality and informality. I have already described the protocol of the Wednesday afternoon manuscript meetings. These ritual performances were always preceded by an equally ritual luncheon—generally at the Ivy Restaurant. Every Wednesday, at a quarter to one, off the five of us would troop—for David Grover had also joined the Board—wending our way along the insalubrious alleys which were prescribed as the essential short cut to our destination, Michael sniffing the dubious atmosphere with delight, O.K. stopping every now and then to inquire after the health and well-being of one of those bundles of rags and misery who then camped out in various dark corners along our route. "My old dears," he called them. He was for ever getting derelicts of this kind into hospital, and going to pay them lengthy and, I should imagine, embarrassed visits when they were there. Arrived at long last at the Ivy—we moved at O.K.'s pace, which became progressively slower and slower—we would settle down to an enormous blow-out at the firm's expense. O.K. belonged to the Savile Club, and Michael to the Garrick, but they were both essentially "restaurant men." They loved restaurants and food and wine—though O.K. ate very little. They always knew the names of headwaiters and waiters, and they enjoyed ordering food, and studying wine lists, and signing bills. In my impatient and intolerant way I found these weekly feasts rather a bore; and though I enjoyed the food I was inclined to regard the whole business as a waste of money. About twice a year, we would abandon a Wednesday manuscript meeting and, instead, go in a body to a matinée. This was always Michael's idea; and the play that he chose was generally a Robertson Hare farce. O.K. used to take a boyish delight in these occasional theatrical jaunts. His day-by-day life must, now I come to think of it, have been dreadfully dull and drab.

Wednesday afternoons apart, if there was an important point to decide—terms for a new book, for instance—we would assemble for an *ad hoc* meeting in the Boardroom. Michael, on these occasions, was remarkably business-like. We were a business-like firm. Otherwise, there was very little *va et vient* between offices. I would go to Michael's room only if I wanted to ask him about something or to tell him something. O.K. would occasionally shuffle along the passage at the end of the day in order, as he used to put it, "to smoke a cigarette with the other two, and have a little chat". For the rest, we remained in our own small kingdoms, getting on with our jobs.

With the exception of O.K., we were all, I think, far too much immersed in detail. This was partly because we enjoyed it, partly because the staff was still very small. Production was my main preoccupation and worry; and Amy Johnston, the production manager, was, fortunately for me, a paragon. At some stage in the war there had been a mysterious blow-up between O.K. and Mr Terry, and Mr T. had left to join another firm. With one of those brilliantly eccentric strokes that he occasionally displayed, O.K. had apparently summoned Amy to his office—she was then head of what might, in a larger establishment, have been called the secretariat—and had blandly informed her that she must forthwith take over Mr Terry's duties. How she had contrived to master the various highly technical processes of her new office I cannot imagine, but she had certainly succeeded. Printers, binders, blockmakers and paper-makers found her an opponent worthy of their steel. I found her a pillar of strength. And if I got out of my depth in trade matters, there was always Mr Bishop. He had been with the firm all his working life. The recognized *doyen* of publishers' representatives, he had by this time retired from the road; but he knew every bookseller in the country, and every book that Constable's had ever published. Very few trade problems ever cropped up that Mr Bishop had not encountered before.

Chapter Seven

AFTER the debacle of *The Hundred of Hoo* I rested on my oars so far as writing was concerned—a dangerous thing to do, for nothing rusts so quickly as a writer's ability to think of something to write about. I do not think that I had been unduly put off by *Hoo's* bad reviews. I soon managed to forget them. But, having developed a passion for playing golf, week-end after week-end slipped away, and an occasional short story (I still found ideas for plots difficult to come by) was about all that I achieved. What I vaguely thought I would like to have on the stocks would be a "general" book which would not involve too much research—something that I could tackle in the evenings at home, and in the train coming back from London. As it was I was apt to fall asleep in my railway carriage as soon as I had finished reading the evening paper, and that seemed a waste of valuable spare time. One morning, before rushing off to the station after breakfast, I stuffed my typed copy of the extracts from Richard Hayes's Diary into my brief-case; and that evening I read it through between Bromley South station and Sole Street. Another die was cast.

Early in 1937, soon after I had married and had come to live at Meadow House at Cobham—which is the next-door village to Meopham where I had been born and brought up—our nearest neighbour, Miss Stevens of the Parsonage, had come to pay a formal call. Very old indeed, she was the last surviving member of a Kentish yeoman family who had owned and farmed a good deal of land in the parish for generations. For something to say I had told our visitor that the architect whom we were employing to carry out some alterations to our house had suggested that it had almost certainly been built in the first quarter of the eighteenth century. Miss Stevens had been visibly shocked. "Oh, no," she said. "I am afraid that he has got his dates *all* wrong. Meadow House was built by Bonham Hayes, Richard Hayes's elder brother, in the year 1771." This was news to me; and I asked the old lady how on earth she could be so certain. It is easy enough as a rule to find out who built great houses, and when. It is far more difficult to ascertain these facts in the case of small houses; and if our caller was right, it meant that yet another provincial builder had used an out-of-date pattern book. "Why," Miss Stevens said, "it's all in Richard Hayes's Diary. In the eighteenth century, you know, Richard Hayes lived and farmed here in the village at Owletts, where Sir Herbert Baker lives now; and he kept a very full diary. Sir Herbert was kind enough to lend me the extracts that his father made from the original diary manuscript; and I had some copies made. I will send one of them over to you this evening." She had been as good as her word, but, beyond looking up the references to the building of my own house, which were conclusive though a bit scanty, I had only flicked through the pages.

I had then had at the back of my mind the foolish conviction that "village history" was rather small beer; and I had often wondered why my scholarly grandfather had bothered on with it. It was all right, I had felt, for parsons and maiden ladies to burrow away in parish registers and manorial records; but for someone like myself there was rather higher historical game to fly at. The first time I had begun to see the error of my ways had been in the summer of 1939. It had taken the imminence of a world war to convert me to the idea that a genuine but uninformed fondness for the countryside over which I had walked and ridden all my life could be strengthened by trying to find out something about it—why its houses, fields, woods and roads were as they were, what they had looked like in the past.

I had not known, during that ominous summer, how many more week-ends I would be allowed to spend among these familiar surroundings. I had not known whether, in a year's time, I should still find myself walking back from Sole Street station on a fine working-day evening through Miss Stevens's cherry orchard to Gold Street, and then on across the church fields by way of Copthorn Shaw. Each morning, as I had put on my clothes, I had wondered how many more times I would enjoy the view of the curved line of Ashenbank Wood from my dressing-room window.

It had been an instinctive effort, I suspect, to identify myself more closely with these places that had led me, then, to read and study the extracts from Richard Hayes's Diary more carefully; and if the war had not come I might have done something about it. Now, the war over, my chance re-reading of the Diary in the train had convinced me that there might "be a book in it."

I should, by rights, have observed warning signals flashing in all directions. As a start, the Diary itself, as I already knew, had been lost. Richard Hayes had owned the substantial seventeenth-century mansion-house called Owletts; and had farmed extensively not only in the parish of Cobham, but also in the neighbouring parish of Meopham, and at Cooling and at Allhallows in the Hundred of Hoo. He had kept a diary covering (with a break of a couple of years in the middle) the period 1760-1788. After the diarist's death in 1790, Owletts and most of the land that went with it had been acquired by the Bakers, of Rochester; and it had been the owner of the Owletts property in the 1890s, Mr T. H. Baker, who had compiled the extracts, a copy of which Miss Stevens had given me.

The obvious inference to draw was that the diary itself had never left the diarist's house; but Sir Herbert Baker, Mr T. H. Baker's son and his successor at Owletts, had assured me that this was not the case. His father, he was certain, had never owned the Diary. He had merely borrowed it for the purpose of making his extracts and, that done, had returned it to its rightful owner. But who that owner had been, and who the present owner was, no one seemed to know. I vainly advertised in the local newspapers, and searched the local libraries and museums; and then, with high hopes, I bombarded my numerous cousins, the descendants of my great-uncle, George Arnold, with inquiries. If the manuscript Diary had ever come on the market during George Arnold's lifetime, the odds were, unless my grandfather had spotted it first, that it would have found its way to Milton Hall, Gravesend.

The branch of the Arnolds to which I belong had established themselves as manufacturers of ships' biscuits at Gravesend as far back as the sixteenth century. It was biscuits of their baking that the East Indiamen which sailed from Tilbury took aboard; and it was their biscuits, I am afraid, that used so regularly to go mouldy and to harbour weevils. In the 1830s my great-grandfather, finding himself in possession of a modest fortune, inconsiderately abandoned his biscuit-making activities, bought two small estates, and set up as a country gentleman. But one of his sons, my great-uncle George, a solicitor with a large and lucrative practice in London, returned in due course to Gravesend, and built himself a large Victorian mansion, Milton Hall, on the outskirts of the town. He was an omnivorous collector, amasser and restorer. Anything that was old and that had any connection with north-west Kent had been grist to his mill. He bought decaying hall houses and restored them, and he restored several disused and decaying chapels. Any monolith or inscribed stone or sarsen boulder that he could lay his hands on he purchased, and set up on the large lawn that fronted Milton Hall. The turf fairly bristled with mysterious monuments of antiquity. On one occasion a man was found trespassing in the grounds. When expostulated with, he said that he was sorry. He had thought it was a churchyard. He tacked two museums on to his house, and filled both of them. He had a remarkable collection of bygone agricultural implements. His library overflowed with local books and papers. He obtained the manuscript diary of an eighteenth-century Gravesend worthy called Robert Pocock, who had been by turns a printer, a botanist, a seller of curios, and a paper-hanger. My great-uncle edited and published this diary. He had fallen out with his youngest brother, my antiquarian grandfather, although they clearly had a great many tastes in common. Great-uncle George had turned Roman Catholic. It was thought best that the brothers should no longer meet; and although they lived within five miles of one another they did not exchange a word for fifty years. I had hoped that great-uncle George might have snapped up Hayes's Diary; but none of his grandsons or granddaughters could find it, and on second thoughts it occurred to me that if it ever had been in his hands he could hardly have resisted the temptation to publish it with an Introduction and Notes—which was exactly what I wanted to do myself. But only, of course, if I could find the original document. The extracts that Mr Baker had made represented a bare half loaf of bread.

I never found the Diary; and I had to be content in the end with a story that it had belonged to some unnamed person in Gravesend, and that it had perished in a fire in the first years of this century. I still live in hopes that it may one day turn up; and, to judge from the quality of the extracts, I still think that, in its entirety, it would be well worth publishing, for it would give a detailed picture of the day-by-day life and interests of a Kentish gentleman farmer in the eighteenth century. It was at this point that I succumbed to temptation—and I am very glad now that I did.

The extracts in my possession were numerous, and some of them were quite long. They had been chosen, clearly, with care and discretion; and their compiler had not only lived in the diarist's house, he had also owned and farmed the self-same land in Cobham. So he should have known what he was about. But the fact remained that they were only extracts and, with however long an Introduction, and however copiously annotated, they would not, as I realized, make a book on their own. But by this time I had found out a good deal about the Hayes family, and Richard Hayes had begun to interest me as a person. And the more I studied them, the more the Diary extracts attracted me. It was fascinating to read of George III being proclaimed King in my own familiar village street by a man on horseback who was the direct ancestor of the owner of the little shop where I regularly bought my cigarettes. It was equally fascinating—or it fascinated me—to discover what crops had been grown nearly two hundred years before in the fields over which I walked most week-ends. Richard Hayes was devoted to Owletts; and many of the extracts from his Diary dealt with the house, its gardens, and its orchards. Whenever I liked I could walk down to present-day Owletts and trace on the ground where the walls and trees and buildings referred to by the diarist had stood. It amused me, for example, to reconstruct the original layout of what the diarist called his "Chessnutt Walk over ye Way". This had been an extension of his pleasure grounds beyond the road on to which the Owletts forecourt faced; and it had consisted of three rows of well-spaced-out horse chestnut trees. The left hand, tree-lined alleyway, which was on the axis of the front door and the forecourt path had, as the extracts from the Diary showed, been planted with clipped yew and box bushes, and at the far end of this walk there had been an obelisk in the Chinese taste, visible from the parlour windows. The last of the chestnuts that Richard Hayes planted was felled a few years back; but the yew and box bushes are still there; and so is the mound on which the obelisk stood.

The village history virus was actively at work in my veins; and I decided, rashly, to use the extracts as part of a wider project. I would try, I decided, to write a book about Cobham.

It was not to be a straightforward history of the village; but a description of what the village was like in 1948, coupled with a picture of what it had been like in 1760; and for the eighteenth century I would draw heavily on the Diary extracts. I should have been deterred by yet another warning signal. Describing a village is one of the most difficult tasks that a writer can set himself. He can compile a straightforward guide-book which can either be factual in its approach, or chatty. Or he can conduct the kind of survey that the children from the Rochester school were to attempt in the still distant future. Neither of these effects was what I was after. I wanted to paint, in words, the picture of a village that would give pleasure to people who had never been near the place, and never intended to visit it; and this, as I should have realized, is an extremely difficult thing to do. A skilled topographical writer can occasionally contrive to describe a landscape, or a town, or a village, or a house so that a reader, although he has never been there, can picture it clearly in his mind's eye. He can walk down that long dusty lane, with the hanging beech wood on his right and the rolling fields on his left. He can tread the urban streets and smell the particular smells of the particular town that are so graphically described. He can walk past the village duck pond, and on round the corner by the elm trees and the thatched timber and wattle cottage. He can mount the steps leading up to the front door of the stately mansion, look back over its park and, with his guide, go through every room in the house. But it needs skill and a lot of practice to achieve descriptive writing of this quality; and I was proposing to take the thing several steps further. As I conducted my reader through present-day Cobham, I intended to invite him to try to imagine what it had all looked like two hundred years earlier. It was an enterprise even more hazardous than *The Hundred of Hoo*; but I am very glad that I undertook it. Regarded as a book, *A Yeoman of Kent* probably failed to come off; but, for all that, it was a respectable try. It was the start of an interest and an enthusiasm which have steadily grown with the years. I should have missed a lot of pleasure if I had never turned village historian. And I was remarkably fortunate in my village.

From as far back as I can remember, Cobham had always

exerted a strong attraction for me. I can just remember, as a very small boy, driving in to Rochester from Meopham by way of Cobham Park. This was an exciting adventure from the word go because, as a rule, we went in the dog-cart, and a dog-cart was the equivalent of today's open sports car. I always looked forward to driving up Cobham Street because we passed the Leather Bottle Inn, where Mr Pickwick had once stayed; and because we were pretty sure to encounter the vicar, the Rev. Arthur Berger, enveloped in an Inverness cape and tricycling very slowly either up or down the hill. Mr Berger held the living of Cobham for more than fifty years, and was splendidly eccentric. As I knew, because we sometimes went to services in Cobham church (my grandfather, by this time, had retired from the Precinct, and lived at Cobhambury), Mr Berger not only read the prayers and preached the sermon, he played the organ as well, which meant that he was for ever in tottering uncertain transit between his prayer-desk, the organ, and the pulpit. My grandfather, who was both deaf and impatient, disliked long sermons. Mr Berger liked to roam round and round his subject. Grandpapa could stand about twenty minutes. After that he would pick up his walking stick and start tapping sharply on the pew. The louder my grandfather tapped, the louder Mr Berger shouted. It was an interesting contest. Either I had been told, or else I must have invented, a mythical story which explained why my grandfather was allowed to behave in this unruly way. Mr Berger, I believed, acted as agent for a firm that supplied a certain kind of tombstone; and he had laid down an edict that anyone who wanted to erect a tombstone in Cobham churchyard must have one conforming to a pattern which could be obtained only from the firm with which he was connected. It was illegal for a clergyman to dabble in trade and commerce. My grandfather had discovered this irregularity; and he might at any moment report the Vicar to the Bishop. This cannot possibly have been true; but it is nevertheless a fact that all the Darnleys who died during Mr Berger's reign were given distinctive Celtic granite crosses and, by way of poetic justice, my grandfather got one too.

After Cobham Street, we bowled down Lodge Lane and into Cobham Park. This was exciting because, first of all, away to the left, there was a glimpse of the south front of the Hall; then, nearly always, a deer or two would jump out of the bracken and make the horse shy; and finally we passed the mausoleum on the top of William's Hill. I was secretly rather frightened of the mausoleum which, as I now know, had been designed by Wyatt in his classical manner. It had been explained to me that a mausoleum was a place in which people were buried; but that no one had ever been buried in the Cobham mausoleum because it had never been consecrated. The Lord Darnley who had built it had insulted the Bishop of Rochester when he had come to conduct this necessary service; and the Bishop had gone straight back to his palace at Bromley in a huff. But I did not altogether trust this tale. I suspected that the building was, in fact, stuffed with dead Darnleys, laid one on top of the other; and that even on a hot summer's day wraith-like ghosts might come floating out through its oddly secular front door, down its flight of stone steps, and through the tall iron railings. I was always relieved when we had safely passed the mausoleum and had plunged into the woods beyond, after unlocking the gate in the deer fence with the key that had been a wedding-present to my father and mother.

Even at a tender age Cobham Hall, and everyone and everything connected with it, had interested me strongly. I was taken to a children's party there one Christmas; and although I was very young I must, already, have been very impressionable. The gilt hall, lit up at night, with its marbled walls, its gilded, elaborately decorated ceiling, its organ, its looped crimson curtains, and the superannuated hop-poles blazing in its enormous fireplace, was probably enough to impress anyone. Lord Clifton, the son and heir of the house, had recently married, and his bride had been much in evidence on this occasion, laughing and talking with a lot of other beautiful and fashionable young ladies from London. They were the first beautiful and fashionable young London ladies I had ever seen and, next morning, when I was being taken for one of our usual walks by my governess, I loitered behind, digging intently in the roadside bank. Commanded to hurry up, I rejoined her, proffering a large lump of chalk. "If," I suggested eagerly, "you rubbed this all over your face you would look like the ladies at Cobham Hall." The suggestion was poorly received. Later, when I was growing up, and when I was a young man, Cobham and Cobham Hall continued to fascinate me. I must have been, indeed I am sure that I was, every kind of a snob—a culture-snob, an Establishment snob, and a thorough-paced social-snob.

My culture-snob centres in Cobham were Cobhambury, where my grandfather lived; and Scalers Hill, the house which my gardener-artist aunt, Winnie Booth, had built in a clearing of the woods behind Chamber's Hill, and where she had made a most lovely garden.

I used greatly to enjoy going to see my grandfather although, by this time, he was extremely old, very deaf, very blind, and excessively impatient of fools. But I surmised, correctly, that he was an expert historian and, in his own quiet way, a distinguished man of letters; and it gave me pleasure and satisfaction to know that he collected books. I could also appreciate that he possessed a sharp tongue and a fund of excellent stories. He had a small library upstairs, where books were double-stacked on the shelves, and where there were more books in piles on the floor and still more in brown paper parcels which he had never got round to opening. But he generally sat in his dining-room, at the end of a long table strewn with papers. He was always writing when I went to see him. As his sight was so bad, what he wrote was generally illegible; but that did not matter. Writing kept him happy. I shall be exactly like that if I ever live to be as old as he was. He used to talk to me about Dr Johnson, about poetry, and about his poet brother, Edwin

Arnold, whom he had loved and admired, but whom he had darkly suspected of writing occasional pot-boilers. *The Light of the World*, for example, that had been so much inferior to *The Light of Asia*. Occasionally he would talk about his young days, when he had been articled to a firm of solicitors in Somerset. There, most improbably as it seemed to me, he had married the daughter of a fox-hunting squire. My grandmother had had a number of brothers all of whom had gone hopelessly to the bad, mostly in connection with the strings of racehorses they had owned. She herself, however, had developed a passion for female education and had founded the Girls' Grammar School at Rochester. I expect that it was from her side of the family that my father derived his love of horses. My grandfather, so far as I know, had never ridden in his life. When I knew him, he had a prehistoric de Dion-Bouton landaulette, driven by his equally antique chauffeur, Crittenden. About twice a year Grandpapa came to luncheon with us at Meopham; and on these occasions the de Dion would stand outside our dining-room windows, dripping oil on the gravel and phut-phutting noisily all through the meal. This was because Crittenden, who was having his lunch in the servants' hall, found the engine hard to start, and preferred to leave it running. Luckily my grandfather was too deaf to detect this subterfuge. The unnecessary consumption of petrol would have pained him very much indeed.

My Aunt Winnie, worldly but at the same time and in her own peculiar way deeply religious, was a pretty good artist and a first-class gardener. She was a friend of Miss Jekyll and of Miss Willmott. Her house, smelling strongly of woodsmoke and containing a good deal of light oak furniture which had been designed and made for it in the early 1900s, seemed in some mysterious way to be an integral part of its garden which, in its turn, merged imperceptibly with the surrounding woods. At Scalers, to my great satisfaction, I was treated from an early age as a sophisticated grown-up. It was taken for granted that I appreciated painting and flowers and books and amusing, slightly malicious conversation. Her way of life also seemed to me to be most enviable, and very different from what I was accustomed to at home. My father's interests were almost exclusively sporting. My mother, whom I adored, spent a great deal of her time, energy and money doing good to others. The arts, in any shape or form, played little part in our daily round. Aunt Winnie had no sporting instincts, and she did things not because she felt that she ought to do them, but because she enjoyed doing them. She loved painting and gardening and going to church, and she loathed the idea of good works in any shape or form. So she painted and gardened and went to church to her heart's content. Her husband, my Uncle Arthur, had the notable distinction in my eyes of having owned the very first private motor-car to be registered in the county of Kent. It had also been a de Dion-Bouton, and in it my uncle and aunt had once set out for the north of Scotland. They had left Scalers at 4 a.m. in order to get through London before there were too many horses on the streets, and my aunt, reckoning that there would be little profit in going to bed for such a short time, had settled herself into the car at midnight. I recalled this epic journey recently when I was hurtling along the fast lane of the Doncaster by-pass at eighty miles an hour. I wish I knew how long it had taken my uncle and aunt in their tiny single-cylinder machine to reach Brora, in Sutherland, which had been their destination. I do know that they got there—and returned safely to Cobham.

My Cobham Establishment-snob centre was Owletts. Sir Herbert Baker, who was then sharing the top of the architectural tree in uneasy conjunction with Sir Edwin Lutyens, was devoted to my grandfather and, as a result, was always particularly kind to me. All manner of interesting people used to come down at the week-ends to stay with him in the handsome house which Richard Hayes's grandfather had built in 1684; and he very often used to ask me over to luncheon or dinner on Sundays. Life at Owletts was conducted on the basis of high thinking and comfortable living. On the comfortable living side there was excellent, rather plain, wholemeal bread and masses of butter and cream kind of food; very good, rather plain, furniture,—some old, some the work of the contemporary craftsmen whom Sir Herbert encouraged; a lot of china, again some old and some the work of potters whom he also befriended; and old family pictures and tapestries alongside the work of modern artists. The high thinking side was conducted against a background of cold baths, church on Sunday mornings, long walks, tree-felling, and strenuous forms of gardening—one of Sir Herbert's ruling passions was clearing and planting an old choked chalk pit in one of his cherry orchards. Reading was encouraged—but only the best books; and there were always oceans of talk—serious, well-informed talk that reflected a tremendous sense of the duty owed to God, to the Country and, above all, to the Empire. Proconsuls, diplomats, cabinet ministers, artists, authors, bishops, editors, headmasters, and heads of colleges at Oxford and Cambridge—all the people who used to stay at Owletts seemed to be great talkers and deep thinkers. Conversations that had begun in the long narrow panelled dining-room were continued after dinner as the guests strolled across the lawn, beside the tall clipped yew hedges and the white glimmering flowers, and on into the old cherry orchards beyond. I used to listen all ears as men who had done great things at home and in every corner of the globe argued, and told stories, and indulged in a rather learned, rather special kind of badinage and chaff. John Buchan, at that time, was my favourite author. At Owletts I felt that I was living in a John Buchan kind of world—indeed he was a friend of my host and so, appropriately, was Rudyard Kipling.

My social-snob centre was Cobham Hall. When I first came to know the great house it was generally deserted. The Lord Darnley of the day—Ivo Bligh, of cricketing and "The Ashes" fame—had built himself a much smaller house nearby; and except when it was occasionally let to a rich American the Hall was empty. I used sometimes to ride over from Meopham, have a gallop in the park, and then tie up my horse and wander through the pleasure grounds that had been laid out by Humphry Repton in 1790. They had a sleeping-beauty kind of charm and mystery. Round nearly every corner there was a temple, or an orangery, or a grotto, or a druids' circle, or a Gothic dairy. Then Lord Clifton, whose first wife I had admired so much, succeeded; and he and his second wife opened up the house again, filling it at week-ends with their friends. Lord Darnley was an exceptionally good-looking giant of a man; and he was nothing by halves. Sometimes he could be alarmingly irritable. At other times he was extremely amusing, kindness itself, and great fun. He was a talented artist and an expert and skilled landscape gardener; but he longed to write plays and act in them himself. He wrote terrible plays, and acted rather badly. Lady Darnley was clever, artistic and full of go. If they were short of a young man, they used to ask me over. On a fine June evening, the great pink brick house was breathtakingly beautiful; and the life that its owners led seemed to me to be tremendously varied and exciting.

I had another, quite different, and more abiding link with Cobham. If my own life at home, though blissfully happy, sometimes seemed a bit restricted and restrained, it involved two exercises which I had always greatly enjoyed. From a very early age I had been accustomed to go for long walks; and I had always been provided first with a succession of ponies, and then with a succession of horses. Very often, as children, we had walked all the way over to tea at Cobhambury or Scalers Hill; and later on my rides had generally been in the direction of Cobham. So I knew, and felt that I had always known, its roads, its lanes, its fields, and its woods; and when, in 1936, I had married and had gone to live at Meadow House, the little red brick house which Richard Hayes's elder brother had built just off Cobham Street, I had felt that in a sense I was coming home. Writing a book about Cobham, I thought, would be like writing a book about someone I had known and loved for a long time. It was only when I came to write it that I discovered how shallow and inadequate my knowledge had really been.

I had imagined that it was going to be an easy book to write; but I was wrong. It involved a tremendous amount of work. I had to find out about farming practice in the eighteenth century —which I enjoyed, because I could go out at any time and walk round the fields and orchards in which the diarist had grown his wheat and his hops and his barley and his cherries. Richard Hayes had served his turn as churchwarden, overseer of the poor, and road surveyor—so I had to do a good deal of the despised burrowing in the parish registers. I had to find out what the church, the college, the Hall, and the public houses in the village had looked like in 1760; and decide which cottages and houses and farmhouses had been there then, and which hadn't. I started endless hares, and duly pursued them. How had cricket been played in the eighteenth century, and how had partridges been shot? How had hops been grown and dried and marketed? What labour force had the diarist employed on his farm, and how much had he paid his farm servants? And then again, trying to paint a picture of the present-day village meant looking at it with new, inquiring eyes; talking to people; and asking endless questions. Delving into the ramifications of the Hayes family entailed looking up old wills in Somerset House; and I spent long evenings poring over old maps, new maps, and old estate plans. At long last, and belatedly, I was doing, or beginning to do, an honest job of local history.

In the course of my researches I had the one statutory stroke of luck that every writer of every book is entitled to. Either Richard Hayes had not written much in his Diary about the economics of his farming activities and about his household expenditures, or else Mr T. H. Baker had thought that these bits were dull, and had failed to copy them out. At all events, in these directions, so far as the Diary extracts went, I had very little to go on. One evening, when Alfred Baker, Sir Herbert's youngest son, was dining with us, I mentioned this troublesome gap. "Have you," he asked me, "ever seen that old Hayes account book? It's in the library at Owletts, and as far as I remember it's full of farming payments and receipts." I had never seen it; and next day he brought me up a fat little vellum-covered book, fastened with a flap and a metal clasp. On its front inside cover was the inscription, "1736. Rich^d. Hayes"; so I knew that it had belonged not to the diarist but to his uncle, Richard Hayes senior. The diarist had been brought up at Owletts by this uncle, and had inherited the property from him in 1754.

The account book was a great help to me. Uncle Richard Hayes had lived in the same house and had farmed the same land as his nephew and namesake; and his financial transactions, as revealed in his detailed and meticulous accounts, cleared up a lot of points which had worried me in the Diary extracts. I was especially interested by Uncle Hayes's dealings in sheep, a word which, incidentally, he always wrote as "Ship". This spelling suggests that "ship" was the current pronunciation, and adds weight to Logan Pearsall Smith's contention (in his book *Words and Idioms*) that the proverb "To spoil a ship for a ha'porth of tar" referred to sheep and not to ships. He generally bought his ewes in October at the famous Weyhill Fair in Hampshire; and they were then driven all the long way back to Cobham.

*   *   *

I wrote two or three chapters of *A Yeoman of Kent* sitting on the terrace of Poggio Gherado, at Settignano, where we were staying with Mrs Aubrey Waterfield. I had come to Italy to see Bernard Berenson, whose book, *Sketch for a Self-portrait*, we were bringing out. I had expected an encounter with a thoroughly formidable author; and I had anticipated a battle royal over the few changes that I wanted to make in the text. I found that in fact Mr Berenson was very small, very fragile, very mild, very talkative and, to my surprise, perfectly amenable.

He in his turn, as he told me, had expected to be confronted by an elderly publisher with a long white beard. I worked away at the *Yeoman* with the view of Florence beyond Mrs Waterfield's sloping vineyards to distract me, with the hot apricot jam scent of *oleo fragrans* to delight me, and when I should, by rights, have been sightseeing. I was never, at the best of times, a very enthusiastic sightseer; and Mrs Waterfield was an omniscient and alarming cross-examiner. Having told us, when we set out, that we must be sure to go to such and such a church in Florence, she would fix us, on our return, with one of her eagle glances. "I take it," she would say, "that you persuaded the priest to show you the little primitive behind the curtain in the sanctuary? You didn't? Oh, but in *that* case it was hardly worth while going there at all, was it?" Sometimes we used to prevaricate and pretend that we had seen things that we hadn't. We were nearly always caught out. I became very fond of our exceptionally intelligent and extraordinarily handsome hostess. Her standards, which were high, may have been infectious. *A Yeoman of Kent* was, I like to think, a better written and a better constructed book than *The Hundred of Hoo*.

Chapter Eight

ONE of the peculiarities of Constable's was how hard everyone, with the exception of O.K., worked. This suited me well enough. I have always thrived on hard work. The only really unhappy times that I have so far experienced in my life have been times when I have had too little to do. Then, inevitably, I found that a law of diminishing return set in—the less I had to do, the less I appeared to be able to do. And a state of general misery, frustration and dissatisfaction resulted.

I expect that there are plenty of skilled and highly successful publishers who sit at tidily bare desks, occasionally ringing someone up, or pressing a bell in order to issue instructions to an assistant. No doubt they think deep thoughts, have brilliant ideas, and are able to see the wood for the trees. Michael, Martha and I were always plunging about in the undergrowth.

When, as happened quite often, some young man just down from Oxford or Cambridge came to see me to inquire how he could "get into" publishing, I used to ask him straightaway whether he was good at figures. A look of pained distaste usually crossed his face. "No," he would say, "I'm afraid that maths were never really my strong point." I would then ponderously explain to him how much of a publisher's time was in fact spent in chasing pennies and halfpennies; and how important such pursuits were. My question was almost certainly an unfair one—for no one in the world could have been stupider about figures than I was. But I never failed to end my homily by telling these aspirants that if they were really determined to become publishers they would certainly succeed. They would, though I did not tell them so, inevitably find that there was someone else in the firm they joined who fancied himself no end at mental arithmetic.

On the lines of our Wednesday afternoon manuscript meetings I had by this time instituted Wednesday morning manufacture meetings, because they saved me a lot of running about between offices in order to get agreed decisions. It was at these Wednesday morning meetings that Amy Johnston, our production manager, used to bring up the estimates for any new books that had recently been put in hand.

These estimates looked, and were, fairly complicated. They set out the cost quoted by the printer for composing and printing each of the books in question, the cost, quoted by the binder, for binding the edition, and what the paper that it would be printed on would come to. Then there were the costs of binding blocks, blocks for the dust jacket, blocks for illustrations, if any, and odds and ends like the wrapper-artist's fee and the indexer's fee, if it had to have an index. From these figures she had arrived at the actual total cost—the money that we would be investing in the undertaking—as well as what each individual copy of the book would cost, bound. To the basic cost per copy, bound, she added the author's royalty on every copy sold; a fixed sum, per copy, as an advertising allocation; and the percentage that we had been told by our accountants that we had to make in order to cover our overheads and by way of profit. Then, knowing the average discount at which the book would be sold, she could arrive at what the "economic" published price ought to be— the price, that is to say, that we ought to ask for the book and that would be printed on the front flap of its jacket. This sounds frightfully complicated, but manufactured goods obviously have to be priced economically by their producer.

Certain production costs—the cost of setting a book up in print, for example, and the costs of illustration and wrapper blocks, remained the same whether the first printing number —the number fixed for the initial printing—was 1,000 copies or 50,000 copies. And so, as a general rule, the higher the first printing number, the lower the cost per copy, bound. This, in its turn, naturally affected the "economic" price at which the book could be brought out; and it was over the pricing of forthcoming books that storms quite often used to break out at our Wednesday morning meetings. All too frequently, in order to keep the published price of a forthcoming book as low as possible, there was a tendency to press for an unduly high first printing number.

Estimating, or rather guessing (because that was what it generally amounted to) what the initial printing number for any given book ought to be was an extremely important art, because a good guess might make all the difference between showing a profit on the transaction or ending up with a loss. If too few copies were printed at the start, a title could easily "go out" while it was still in demand, and then, while it was being hastily reprinted, and while this second impression was being bound, the demand might mysteriously dry up and disappear. This would result in almost the whole of the second impression sitting unsold either in the stockroom or at the binder's—and bang would go the profit that had been made on the first printing. If, on the other hand, the guess had been too optimistic and if, say, 1,000 copies of the first printing remained unsold, once again the transaction as a whole might show a loss. Guessing first printing numbers was something that O.K. was extremely good at. I always imagined that he relied partly on long experience and partly on a kind of sixth publishing sense. And at any given time he had a pretty good idea of how sales trends were going, because he simply loved opening and sorting out the daily orders himself—a practice which I, in my superior wisdom, used to consider a great waste of time. He was right in his guesses far oftener than any of the rest of us, and he retained this skill right up to the end.

For argument's sake, let us suppose that on a certain Wednesday morning estimates for an average-length detective novel by a new author came up for consideration. Our job was to decide on the first printing number for this book, and to fix its published price. Amy would have duly worked out the costs for first printing numbers of, say, 2,000, 2,500 and 3,000 copies; and these might show that if we started away with 2,000 copies the book's "economic" published price would have to be 11s. 6d.; if we printed 2,500 it would have to be 11s.; and if we printed 3,000 it could be as low as 10s. 6d.

Each of us round the table would then give his or her idea of what the initial printing number *ought* to be, irrespective of the published price. Michael and I, and possibly Martha, would have read the book in question in manuscript. O.K. might or might not have "glanced through" it. But O.K.'s guess as to how many we would be likely to sell would probably be the soundest. And he might guess 2,000 copies. This would put the cat among the pigeons because Amy's figures showed that if we only printed 2,000 copies the published price would have to be 11s. 6d.

At any given time, so far as "general" books were concerned, there was usually a certain amount of room for manœuvre in the matter of published prices. It did not matter very much whether a travel book or a biography was published at 20s. or at 18s. But published prices for novels, and especially for detective stories and thrillers, were nearly always "fixed". There was a price at which the library buyers would buy this class of fiction, and beyond which they would not go. Let us suppose that the ruling price for detective fiction was 10s. 6d. This being the case, we were obviously on the horns of a dilemma. We wanted to print 2,000 copies of this particular whodunnit; but at that number its "economic" price would have to be 11s. 6d.

When a book had got as far as the estimates stage, it usually had a sponsor. Either Michael and Martha, generally acting in concert, would have backed it strongly when it had come up at a manuscript meeting, or else I would have been keen on it.

And it was at this point in the proceedings that the sponsor would take fright.

If, he would argue, "his" book came out at 11s. 6d.—which in any case was a silly price—no one would buy it. It would fall as flat as a pancake. The right price was 10s. 6d.—and 10s. 6d. it jolly well must be. So he would proceed to go into battle. Seizing the estimates book from Amy, and having tried, unsuccessfully, to prove that she had made mistakes in her arithmetic, he would study the figures and announce that the prices quoted were far too high. The cost for composition, for example. Ridiculous! Amy, never at a loss, would explain that she had obtained no fewer than three prices from three different printers. The one quoted was the lowest. Well, then, what about the binding cost? Far too high! And the cost of paper? Monstrous! Amy would patiently explain that she *could* knock a halfpenny or two off the cost of binding by using an inferior cotton cloth, and save another penny or two on the cost per copy by printing the book on a wood-pulp paper, but—eyeing Michael—she did not think that Mr Sadleir would be very happy with the look of the finished book. *And,* she would add, there would be quite an appreciable saving if the dust jacket could be printed in line in two colours; but she had estimated for four-colour half-tone blocks, because she understood that Mr Sadleir had already passed the artist's rough for the cover.

Routed in these directions, the sponsor would then try another tack. It was, he would argue, a pretty good detective story. If we really felt that we could not sell more than 2,000 copies of a first-rate detective story we did not deserve to stay in business. This was a vulnerable line of argument, because O.K. would then send for the sales book, and would point out that we had published an equally promising detective novel earlier in the year of which we had, to date, sold 1,800 copies; and conditions in the trade were, if anything, deteriorating rather than improving. The right number, in his view, was either 2,000 or possibly 1,500.

124

Foiled again, the sponsor would fire the last shot left in his locker. If, he would argue, we brought this wretched book out at 11s. 6d.—it had become "a wretched book" by this time—it would not stand a chance, and we should lose a packet of money. If, on the other hand, we printed 2,000 copies, and deliberately under-priced it at 10s. 6d., and if we sold out our first printing quickly, we should be certain of getting our capital outlay back, even if we made no profit at all. And then, if the book caught on, we should be able to slip a quick reprint through and make a decent profit on the second impression. This specious and dangerous argument had been heard all too often before, and it would be the signal for a great deal of activity round the Board-room table. O.K. would ring for Bates and demand his ready-reckoner; and Martha and David Grover, both of whom prided themselves on their heads for figures, would start scribbling on bits of paper. And while O.K. arrived at one set of calculations from his ready-reckoner, and David and Martha arrived at entirely different results from their scribblings and pencil nibblings, Michael and I, who were both completely un-mathematical, would sit back and twiddle our thumbs. The final upshot of all these efforts would be, we knew from experience, hopelessly unreassuring. Once a book was under-priced, it took the whale of a big second printing to catch up.

Generally, the wrangle that followed would end in a compromise. We would decide to print 2,500 copies, bind up 2,000, and price the book at 10s. 6d., thereby almost certainly ensuring that we should get the worst of both worlds. We would probably land ourselves with a lot of surplus copies which, in the end, would have to be "remaindered" at a price below the actual cost of production; and even if, by some lucky chance, we succeeded in selling the whole of our first printing, we would still have made less than our "proper" profit. It was all the fault, we would tell each other bitterly, of the "big boys" who refused to face putting up the prices of *their* books in the face of steeply rising production costs.

This was one of the things I had in mind when I used to tell the young hopefuls who came to see me that quite a lot of their time, if and when they became publishers, would be spent chasing pennies and halfpennies. I also used to tell them that they would spend far less time reading manuscripts and entertaining lady authors to luncheon at the Savoy Grill than they would in trying to sell the end product.

The whole business of selling books, as I had discovered as the result of the supervision that I was supposed to exercise over our trade department, was bedevilled by the fact that every fortnight throughout the publishing seasons—which were growing more and more elastic—we ordinarily brought out two or more brand new products. If cigarette manufacturers, or the producers of bottled beer, had been faced with a similar problem they would probably have given up in despair. We had to grin and bear it.

Any forthcoming book, bearing the imprint of a respectable and respected publishing house, was bound to sell some copies "on subscription"—before, that is to say, it was actually published. How many copies any given book "subscribed" depended on how well known its author was, and on whether or not the travellers had an adequate "talking point" when they took round either finished copies or proof copies to show to booksellers. A new general book, or a new novel, by a well-established and popular writer was, relatively speaking, a piece of cake. Booksellers would happily order it in quite large numbers because they knew in advance that it would have a good sale. A general book or a novel by an unknown author was a much stickier proposition. In the category of general books there were supposed to be "good" subjects and "bad" subjects. In travel books, for instance, a book about Tibet, quite irrespective of its merits, would generally subscribe better than a book about Norway. Much the same thing applied in the case of fiction writers. A "first" detective novel by an Oxford don would stand a better chance than a "first" detective novel by an elderly lady living at Shoeburyness. The saddest and most predictably fallacious statement that was frequently made by authors to their publishers was: "I am certain that my book will subscribe well, because I have simply hundreds of friends scattered all over the country, and I know that they have *all* been bombarding their booksellers to stock it." I always had a sneaking fear that one day we might launch a book that would subscribe no copies at all. We never did.

Once a book was published, its sales, I came to the conclusion, depended on people reading it, liking it, and recommending it to their friends. Starting the ball rolling was the difficulty. In order to have a fair chance, a new book somehow had to be got reasonably quickly into the hands of a reasonably large number of reasonably widely dispersed readers. Extensive pre-publication advertising was usually economically impossible—and in any case would have done little or no good. Reviews were the best and surest way of drawing potential readers' attentions to a new book; and publisher and author alike devoutly hoped for the right review by the right reviewer in the right place in the right paper at the right time. The "right review by the right reviewer" was not, necessarily, a review by Raymond Mortimer or Harold Nicolson, or Cyril Connolly—though such a notice could sell a first impression right out in a week. On the other hand, a book that had been lucky enough to get this treatment might still sell very few copies indeed. Everything depended on what the review said. However long and elegantly phrased, however eminent the reviewer's name, and however impressive the circulation of the paper in which the review appeared, if it made the book sound pretty dull, a review was useless from the point of view of sales. A quite short anonymous review, on the other hand, might do the trick. I remember an instance when a single sentence in a brief, unsigned notice tucked away in a corner of a literary weekly with a small circulation started a book selling. For some reason, that one sentence struck home, and persuaded enough readers that this was a book that they would probably enjoy. Occasionally a hostile review was worth a dozen favourable reviews—if, for example, it suggested that a book was scandalous, or unusually dirty, or sensational in some other way.

Whether a book was reviewed at all was often a chancy business. A new book by a popular author—popular, that is to say, with the reviewers—automatically got widely and promptly reviewed. Ironically, it was this kind of book that needed reviews least. The book that used to worry me most was the book by an unknown or little-known author that, given half a chance, might do very well indeed. But would it get half a chance?

Review copies of all general and fiction titles were always sent some three weeks ahead of publication to the literary editor of every newspaper and weekly that carried a book page. What happened after that was in the lap of the gods. In any given week all through the year most literary editors customarily received far more books for review than they could possibly handle. So there had to be a process of weeding out. Either the literary editor himself—or so I always imagined—picked out the titles that he thought looked interesting and worthwhile; or his reviewers wandered into his office and made their own selections from his shelves. It was a case of many being called and few chosen; and it might be a matter of luck whether a new book by an unknown author was taken down or left. When a fiction reviewer had picked two or three "musts" or "probables" he might, for his remaining choices, be guided by a publisher's imprint, a persuasive blurb, or a striking dust jacket.

It has always been the custom of publishers to grumble about the state of book reviewing at any given time. I used to grumble like mad—but I seldom had any legitimate grounds for complaint. If it was accepted that luck entered into it, by and large the book that deserved good reviews generally seemed to get them. And I never came across a single case where the literary editor of a reputable newspaper or weekly was influenced, or appeared to be influenced, by a publisher's advertising policy. Of course, strings were quite often pulled both by authors and by publishers. If an author knew a reviewer, the chances were that that reviewer, when his friend's book came along, would ask for it and see that he got it. But this worked both ways, for if the reviewer disliked the book, and wanted to keep his friendship intact, then no review would appear, and it was an old saying in the trade that any review of a book was better than no review at all. A publisher might, quite legitimately, tip off a friendly literary editor or a reviewer about a forthcoming book. If it was known that these tips were reliable, then this system worked. If tips from any source proved to be consistently misleading, more harm than good would result from this practice. Constable authors could have rested assured of one thing—we awaited reviews of their books with just as much anxiety as they must have felt themselves. Even now I experience a slight sinking of the heart when I open my newspaper at the book page on a Sunday morning.

People have sometimes asked me how it is that books that are complete flops ever come to be published. Surely, they say, publishers, with all their experience, must have realized that such-and-such a book would never succeed?

Sometimes, of course, the answer is that an author has "sold" his publisher an idea, and the book, when it eventually comes along, is a sad disappointment—but not quite bad enough to justify breaking the agreement to publish it. Sometimes a good writer has an off-day; and having failed to persuade its writer to put the manuscript in question away in a drawer and forget about it, the publisher brings it out because he is afraid that someone else will if he doesn't. But more often, I suspect, the answer is to be found in the operation of a kind of mass hypnotism. Someone in the firm likes something in a manuscript, and contrives—just as a reviewer can sometimes contrive—to fire everyone else's enthusiasm. Glaring faults and obvious disadvantages are conveniently overlooked; and up the rocket goes—only to return to earth with a bump which could have been, and should have been, foreseen.

The two annual occasions which I really dreaded were our travellers' meetings. We held one at the beginning of August and the other at the beginning of January. At the August meeting we went through our forthcoming autumn books with our representatives; in January we told them about our spring books. In theory, our "autumn list" was supposed to be ready in time for the August meeting, and our "spring list" in time for the one in January. They seldom were. All our travellers assembled and sat expectantly round the Boardroom table, in company with the directors (less, sometimes, O.K., who had funked it), Amy Johnston, and our trade manager.

Publishers' representatives are, as a rule, exceptionally intelligent men, and exceptionally nice; but they belong to a race apart—though all travellers, whether they travel in ladies' underclothes, sweets, agricultural implements, or books may, for all I know, be brothers under the skin. Once a publisher's representative always a publisher's representative. If we had a vacancy in the trade department for which it was essential to get the best possible man, I used in my ignorance to try to persuade one of our country travellers to fill it. I imagined that he would snatch at the chance of abandoning arduous days spent in travelling from one place to another only to be kept waiting by reluctant booksellers, and dreary nights away from home spent in uncomfortable provincial hotels. But not at all. None of them would ever contemplate quitting his life on the road.

Publishers' representatives are born deflaters of publishers' pretensions. I used to start each of these travellers' meetings in a spirit of bonhomie and good cheer. I was genuinely fond of each of our representatives individually, and delighted to encounter them *en masse*. And I probably thought, on each occasion, that we had rather a good lot of prospective books to offer them. I was soon disillusioned. The cherished swans, which

Michael or I described to them so enticingly, were quickly cut down to their proper goose status. If we had succeeded in getting hold of a first-class travel book about Tibet, we would be told that booksellers' shops were, at that very moment, crammed with books about Tibet which they were completely unable to shift. If we had what we regarded as a sure-fire best-selling "first" detective novel by an eminent Oxford don, first one traveller and then another would observe that it was a funny thing but Mr So-and-So and Mr Somebody Else had passed the remark only a few days back that he hoped Constable's would not be stuck with another Oxford detective story, because they had had their day and were now a drug on the market. If, by some amazing chance, we succeeded in kindling their guarded enthusiasm for a forthcoming title then, as sure as fate, one of them would inquire what its published price was going to be. "Eighteen shillings, sir? *Eighteen* shillings? Oh, of course, at *eighteen shillings* it won't stand a chance. That's right, isn't it, Mr Blank?" And, as his colleague who covered Scotland and the northern counties nodded lugubrious agreement, I would recall the frightful tussle we had had on a recent Wednesday morning to get the price of this particular book down from 21s. If they thought well of a novel, then its wrapper, when Michael Sadleir proudly produced it for their inspection, would scuttle any chances it had of selling. Or the book itself would be too thin. Unless Constable's books were bulked, we would be told, they did not stand an earthly chance. "You would like them, I take it," Amy Johnston would inquire with acid sweetness, "printed in future on blotting paper?" Even the ebullient Mr Ernie Vines, our town traveller, lost his fanatical enthusiasm on these occasions. But I knew that he and the rest of the travellers would have very different stories to tell about these despised books of ours once they had got back on to the road.

It was inevitable, I suppose, that in course of time and like so many Fellows of Oxford colleges I should try my hand at a full-length detective novel. I had always been a great reader of detective stories; I optimistically imagined that the discipline of a detective story plot would provide a much needed stiffening to the brand of social comedy that I enjoyed writing; and the challenge of "anything you can do, I can do better" operated powerfully. I did not for one moment suppose that I could write half as good a detective novel as, say, Michael Innes or Ngaio Marsh—let alone a better one. But I thought it would be fun to have a shot.

If I had run true to earlier form, my chosen medium would have been the thriller. It had been from thrillers, at one period of my life, that I had largely based my idea of what I should like to do when I grew up. These aspirations were apt to change as I switched from author to author. Under the influence of "Sapper" and Bulldog Drummond, for example, I was all for an uncomplicated life of sport and adventure. Under the influence of Dornford Yates, and taking my cue from Boy Pleydell and Jonah Mansel, I saw myself as equally adventurous but more sophisticated, more a man of the world, and much more of a ladies' man. I would also be excruciatingly witty, constantly causing my friends and relations to double up in paroxysms of uncontrollable laughter. My Buchan-inspired world was a bit more complicated because I could never make up my mind whether I wanted to model myself on Richard Hannay or on Edward Leithen. On the whole I favoured Leithen.

But I refuse to allow myself or anyone else to laugh at John Buchan's self-styled "shockers." In my view he was the master, with a master's touch. His stories race along; he could draw exactly the kind of characters that thrillers need; and when he wanted to he could run rings round most serious character-novelists—as witness *Sick Heart River*. And then he was a past-master at what I always think of as "the hurried journey"; and he was exceptionally good at descriptions of the countryside. "The road led through a great wood of beeches and then into a shallow valley with the green backs of the downs peeping over

132

the distant trees. After Scotland, the air smelt heavy and flat, but infinitely sweet, for the limes and chestnuts and lilac bushes were domes of blossom. Presently I came to a bridge, below which a clear stream flowed between snowy beds of buttercups. A little above it was a mill; and the lasher made a pleasant cool sound in the summer dusk. . . ." He was describing the valley of the Kennet, but whenever I read this passage from *The Thirty-nine Steps* I am taken straight back to the Oxfordshire countryside as I remember it in the months of May and June. Buchan's plots may sometimes have been a bit on the thin side; and there may have been a bit too much of "We climbed five sets of stairs to a flat away up in Montmartre where I was talked to by a fat man with spectacles and told various things that greatly concerned me . . ."; but his craftsmanship was superb. And he *could* write.

If I could have produced a decent, workmanlike thriller I should have been proud and happy. I had had a shot at writing one before the war. I re-read it the other day. It was unutterably bad; and possibly the publisher's blurb on its dust jacket may still further have tended to confuse the mind of anyone unwise enough to have tackled it. The action was described as taking place "in the Highlands of Scotland" whereas, in fact, no character ever ventured north of Dumfries. And the rumblings off-stage were described as happening in the Balkans. They actually took place in China. But no blurb, however accurate and persuasive, could have done much for this lamentable story. Another mistake was that I had evidently tried very hard to write it "in the Buchan tradition." There is nothing that is wrong, and everything that is right, with the Buchan tradition when it comes to thrillers. Personally, I much prefer the amateur who embarks unwillingly on adventures to the hard-boiled professional who is all the fashion at the moment. But nothing to my mind damns a thriller more decisively than a claim by its publisher that it is "in the John Buchan tradition" or "in the Ian Fleming tradition." It ought to be in its own tradition.

So I left thrillers alone, and embarked on a detective story. Detective stories meet a great human need. I do not always want to read them. Sometimes I go for long periods without reading one. But when the mood comes over me, nothing else will do. I have often wondered why this is. I am not particularly interested in the "whodunnit" aspect, though detective stories would be as nothing without this element. I hardly ever spot the murderer and, if I have my suspicions, they nearly always turn out to be misdirected. And I am not above having a surreptitious look at the last few pages. I suspect, when all is said and done, that I like detective novels because their authors have to stick to firm and fast rules, which give their books a proper shape and form; because very often they introduce me to interesting, specialized settings like Oxford colleges, or ladies' hairdressing salons, or solicitors' offices; and because they are frequently better written, less pretentious, and generally much more readable than ordinary novels. I am also very much attached to detectives.

In theory, since I am intensely curious about what people are really like, and how they behave, and why they behave as they do, I should have enjoyed being a detective myself. I should have welcomed a summons to leave my office in Scotland Yard on a sultry afternoon in July to drive down to a large house in Somerset where a baffling murder had been committed. I should have revelled, again in theory, in reading strangers' letters, poking round strangers' houses, searching through their drawers, exploring their cupboards, and ransacking their attics. I should have enjoyed summoning my suspects one by one to the library after dinner, drawing them out, putting them at their ease, getting them off their guard, setting traps for them, and extracting the truth out of each of them in turn. And I should have thoroughly enjoyed jotting down the information I had collected in those neat, logical columns. The next best thing to being a detective in real life is meeting detectives in books.

Again, I have always had an unfulfilled longing to be an expert—a recognized expert in anything. Publishers are never recognized as experts. Authors are nearly always convinced that they know quite as much about the business of publishing as the people who spend their lives at it. Printers regard publishers as ignoramuses. Booksellers are certain that they could do the job a lot better. Chartered accountants smile sadly, as they might if they were dealing with children, when they have anything to do with publishers. During the war I used to envy experts very much indeed. They lived detached, seemingly carefree lives. Very senior officers listened with respect to what they said. They came, they pronounced judgement, and they went away. Detectives are experts in their own specialized field. I should dearly have loved to have had a specialized field.

After *The Yeoman of Kent* I wrote three full-length detective novels in a row. The first was set in a villa on an Italian lake; the second and third had traditional English country-house settings. The Italian one, I like to think, broke new ground because it described what appeared at first sight to have been an attempt to bring off a "murder by suggestion". The amateur detective in it was the same little nursery gardener who had figured in my "Garden Mad" short story. In the second and third books the detecting was done by a Chief Constable, who was by no means such a bumbling old ass as he appeared to be. One of the troubles was that I could never bring myself to introduce any really nasty characters into these stories.

Not long ago I re-read *Fish and Company*, the first of the trio, because it was going to be reissued in a paperback edition. I was amazed to discover that, despite the endless wrestlings I had endured with the intricacies of its complicated plot, I was quite unable to remember who, in fact, *had* committed the murder, and how he had managed it. I had to indulge in one of my surreptitious peeps at the last chapter. In many ways I wish I had gone on writing detective stories. They sold quite well; one a year would have been a nice side-line; and I might have got better at them with long practice. If I ever write another novel it will almost certainly be a detective story.

Chapter Nine

IN the toils of coping with internal office problems in Orange
Street I was sometimes apt to forget that success in publishing
depended, ultimately, on getting the right books, and on getting
on with authors. The process of getting the right books had
changed, and was changing.

O.K. belonged to the era and to the school which had
believed that the publisher's imprint was all-important. An
author who knew his onions would be proud and pleased to have
his book published by Constable's. A literary agent who knew
his business would automatically send a promising manuscript
round to Orange Street. Occasionally word might get about in
the club that an eminent elder statesman was thinking of writing
his memoirs. Then the thing to do was either to approach him
through a mutual friend, or write him a letter expressing polite
interest, or write him a business-like letter offering him a sum
of money down as an advance against royalties. A publisher
used his *savoir faire* and his sixth sense in deciding which of these
courses he should follow. Someone might mention that an
important book was shortly to be published in America. A
stately letter was written to the friendly president of the Boston
publishing house which was to bring it out. He would reply
that he had, of course, always had Constable's in mind for it.
Once in a blue moon, apparently, it had been advisable to move
quickly. The chance presented itself of buying the copyright of
a book that had immense possibilities. A few sums were done
on the back of an envelope, and one of the firm's principals

"went down to the City" and raised £3,000. The accruing profits and prestige were enormous.

I do not for a moment suppose that publishing was ever really in the least like that. But I am quite prepared to believe that, while competition for good books was brisk, the pace of the whole proceeding, in O.K.'s hey-day, was a good deal slower than it was after the First World War; and I am most certainly prepared to believe that when a manuscript was delivered to a publisher, as a general rule he either accepted it as it stood, or rejected it. There was no question, then, of extensive editorial changes carried out in the office—changes that might amount to a virtual rewriting of the whole book. And it was left to printers' readers to correct mistakes and to query facts and points of grammatical usage in the marked proof—and occasionally, in those happy, far-off days, printers' readers were superannuated university dons.

Michael, as I had soon discovered, belonged to a newer school—a school which recognized that there were all too few good books being chased by all too many publishers; and that while a publisher's imprint might be his most valuable possession, it was liable to tarnish if he sat at his desk waiting for manuscripts to fall from heaven. If Michael lighted on a good subject for, say, a Victorian biography, he would search about until he had found someone to write it; and when the manuscript came in, he would spend days and weeks, if it seemed desirable, revising, cutting, and editing it. He was prepared to woo literary agents, recognizing that more and more authors were represented by agents, and that agents, being human, sent their occasional plums to publishers with whom they were on good terms. And he kept in very close touch with American publishers. He was of the opinion, and he may well have been right, that by and large American novelists had more go and fire than their British contemporaries; and he was well aware that it was fatal to sit back and wait for friendly New York and Boston publishers to think of Constable & Company every time they signed an agreement with a new, promising author. Dos Passos was one enthusiasm; and Damon Runyon was another. Runyon, one of whose books had been published over here by someone else and had fallen as flat as a pancake, was a roaring success; and we were subjected to a good deal of Runyonese. He suited one of the quirks of Michael's humour. Another quirk was his passion for giving everyone nicknames. And certain authors were always referred to as "Little" So-and-so. Some of these "little" people were immensely tall.

Relations with authors, if what O.K. told me was to be believed, had changed, too. I gained the impression that, in his day, there had been a few giants in the land—writers like George Meredith and, of course, Shaw in his splendid prime, and later Dreiser. These men had been treated like gods. There had been some best-selling lady novelists, welcome additions to any publisher's list. They had been treated with an amused gallantry. There had been good, sturdy professional men of letters, literary critics, and fellows of Oxford and Cambridge colleges, who could be relied on, in return for very modest rewards, to suggest and edit series, and to write books which, if they did not set the Thames on fire, at least added lustre and body to the firm's backlist. And there had been innumerable minnows. If one of these minnows had had the temerity to come in person to Orange Street he would have been lucky, I gathered, if he got ten minutes with the firm's Reader. Certainly no director would have bothered to see him.

O.K. continued to follow this tradition. He would put himself out (not a thing that he usually cared to do), and go to any pains, for Shaw, or Harold Nicolson, or Helen Waddell, or Lord Vansittart, or Sir Charles Dodds, or Freddie Voigt, or for any of his other heroes or heroines; but it would have been a hardy minor author who would have dared to ring him up to complain that his aunt had tried in vain to buy a copy of his latest book at her local bookseller's. Michael's approach was rather different. He was no hero-worshipper. Indeed on the

138

whole he was a hero-decrier. If he liked an author he would do anything for him, and it did not matter a straw if that author was eminent or obscure. I used to think that Patrick Hamilton and Bruce Marshall, who could always make him laugh, were his favourites. If he did not like an author—and again he might be either a successful or an unsuccessful writer—he could be, and often was, curiously remote and chilling. To be an author in Michael's good books was an enviable situation.

By rights, after I had joined the Constable Board, I should have represented the very latest school in my methods of getting the right books, in my methods of getting new authors, and in my methods of getting on with authors already on the Constable list.

The day of the "thought-up" book—the big anthology or annual that was devised and often executed in the publisher's office—was dawning; and so was the day of the huge, elaborate, and expensive art book. A "handsome package" was beginning to be a better sales gambit than a good-looking book. I should have been alive to these trends; and I should, I suppose, have thought up anthologies, and assembled a fat shiny volume of Picasso reproductions. But I knew that both O.K. and Michael would have damned such projects as "arrant bits of book-making"; and I felt rather the same way myself. Much more importantly, as the youngest member of the Board, I should have had my ear nearest the ground and, looking back, I suspect that I should have advocated, or tried to advocate, that we should radically change our whole publishing policy. We were general publishers, with a sound list of advanced technical, scientific, and medical books. If I had been far-seeing when I came back after the war, or if I had had a lucky session with a crystal ball, I should have foreseen that with the spread of education at home and overseas school text-books were the thing to go for, and I should have done my damnedest, as soon as paper became available, to propel Constable's into the school text-book field. It would not have been easy. We might well

139

have failed. Competition would have been fierce from the start, we should have needed another experienced educational director to look after this enterprise, and we should have had to find a lot of fresh capital. But it would probably have been the right thing to have done. That I did not press for anything of the kind was due to the fact that general publishing was what I liked and enjoyed; and I knew next to nothing about educational publishing.

As far as getting new authors went, I failed in exactly the same way as, up to a point, O.K. and Michael failed, though, earlier on, both had excelled in this art. O.K., at one time, had moved in leftish intellectual circles, going, as he often used to tell me, for long walks with Ramsay MacDonald across Hampstead Heath; and Michael, at one time, had known all the *avant garde* writers like Katherine Mansfield and T. S. Eliot. I was never any good at this side of the business. Socially, I was hopelessly lazy and unambitious. By this time my wife and I had a flat in London, where we spent the middle of most weeks, going down to Cobham at week-ends. From this base I should have sallied out evening after evening to attend literary cocktail parties, literary dinner parties, and the soirées given by literary societies. When I was not engaged in this treadmill round we should have been giving dinner parties ourselves for authors, for prospective authors, for people who knew prospective authors, for literary critics, for literary agents, for literary editors, and for visiting American publishers. At week-ends, we should have entertained a judicious selection of these important people in the country. I failed lamentably in these directions. I did not want to go out, or to have people in, every evening. I enjoyed it much more when old friends, rather than comparative strangers or chance acquaintances, came down for the week-end. I was still fascinated by people who wrote books; but I did not care for them so much *en masse*; and I did not much like literary hangers-on. There was nothing I enjoyed more—and nothing I imagine that my unfortunate wife dreaded so much—as an evening at the flat when an author I was fond of, or a critic I respected, or an agent who was a friend, or a congenial English or American publisher, or a gossipy literary editor came to dinner, and we could indulge in an orgy of publishing and writing shop. But in the ordinary way the idea of living, breathing and eating publishing repelled me. I wanted to have a quiet life of my own outside the office. A successful practitioner of the art—as opposed to the practice—of publishing has no life and precious few thoughts outside publishing. This is a sobering reflection.

I am also guiltily conscious of my failure to play any useful part in the higher counsels of my profession. Michael, so far as I am aware, never—at least when I knew him—attended a single meeting of the Publishers' Association. He would as soon have gone to a race meeting. While I was a perpetual apprentice O.K., once in a blue moon, used to take me with him to one of these gatherings—he would certainly never have gone by himself. And I did, on one occasion, get on to my feet and make a halting contribution to the proceedings. I probably spoke out of turn. At all events I was well snubbed for my pains. I should have persevered, for the Publisher's Association is a body with a considerable potential for good. The trouble is that most publishers are, by nature and by inclination, individualists. They cooperate splendidly when they all find themselves in a deep hole, or when the subject of their deliberations is comparatively unimportant. When it comes to matters like an all-round increase in the published prices of books, or the adoption of a common policy on some question concerned with authors' terms, they are apt to prefer to go their own sweet ways.

Getting on with Constable authors was quite a different story. In theory, the publisher-author relationship ought to be an ideal one. If an author's book does well, both author and publisher benefit. I always found that, in the case of a best-seller, the profits made by the publisher, and the royalties earned by the author, came out in the end just about square. If a book does badly, both parties suffer grievous disappointment. The publisher stands to lose quite a lot of money, and the author stands to earn very little. In practice, I discovered that if a book did extremely well, its author, unless he was a remarkably level-headed person, was subjected to exceptional strains and stresses. Success might go to his head, and he might become inordinately greedy, unreasonable, and demanding. He might be wooed, either directly or through his agent, by other publishers who, on occasion, would not be above suggesting that the success that he had enjoyed would be nothing to the success that he could enjoy if he entrusted his next book to them. Such an author might be downright ungrateful, forgetting the string of unsuccessful books, on which his publisher had lost money, which had preceded the one that had hit the jackpot. He might decide conveniently to forget all the work that his publisher had put in on his last book, work which—though he would probably deny it—had contributed materially to its success.

In my experience the easiest author to deal with was the author who enjoyed a steady, unspectacular success. The most trying author was the author who was consistently unsuccessful, but whose work had a quality and a promise that encouraged persistence. The relationship then smacked of patronage; and it was terribly hard for the publisher-patron not to be patronizing, and for the author not to feel patronized. It did not matter, perhaps, keeping him waiting for a quarter of an hour when he came round to the office; he would not mind being taken to luncheon in that cheapish little restaurant in Soho; and there was really no need to listen to a long string of complaints over the telephone. Authors, successful or unsuccessful, were, I found, understandably sensitive. It was the fate of their brain-children, conceived in rapture and brought forth with prolonged labour and agony, that was in the balance. With each new book they were the victims, inevitably, of delusive and probably false hopes; spinners, time and again, of tantalizing dreams. Authors, I observed, were also subject to frequent fits of jealousy.

Publishers, though authors seldom appreciate it, are also sensitive plants. The failure of a book, especially if it happens to have been a book that he himself had sponsored, possibly against the views of his colleagues, can represent a bitter personal failure to the publisher involved. He may be inclined, then, to put the blame, unfairly, on its writer; and he is in no mood to tolerate an author's reproaches, open or veiled. He can be deeply hurt if an author leaves him to go to another firm. A bad and damaging review of a book that has come out under his imprint is a slur both on his own and on his firm's good name—and is bitterly resented.

Advances against royalties, as I discovered to my cost, could be a fruitful source of friction between authors and publishers. Both in theory and in practice such payments are perfectly proper and sensible. Writing a book generally takes quite a long time. Nowadays, nine months can easily elapse between a book's acceptance and its publication—though when I first went to Constable's we could, when pushed, bring out a novel in three weeks flat. And, thanks to a well-established idiosyncrasy of publishers' accounting, an author whose book is published in February will have to wait for his first royalty statement until the following October. Faced with delays of this kind authors often were—and still are—extremely short of money; and a lump sum down in anticipation of royalties, paid half on acceptance and half on the day of publication, and calculated on a guess as to what the book in question is likely to earn within, say, the first three months of its life, is a practical and reasonably generous method of bridging an ugly gap. But "advances" were all too often made the touchstones of publisher-author relationships. This publisher was said to be "good"—not because he produced nice-looking books and invariably took immense trouble over selling them, but because he could be touched for whacking advances. That publisher was said to be "bad"—not because his production was often shoddy and careless and because he believed in hit-or-miss promotion, but because he displayed a reasonable caution in the advances that he paid. No one seemed to consider that the so-called "good" publisher probably had a list of unearned advances—books, that is to say, that had never earned their advances—as long as his leg; or that the authors who had dealings with a so-called "bad" publisher could look forward, sometimes, to receiving nice fat royalty cheques over the years.

It is easy to be smug over this whole business of advances. An author obviously has one point of view, and a publisher another. A small advance can be taken by an author as a slap in the face, implying that his publisher does not rate his ability or the chances of his book very highly; and a publisher who, wisely or unwisely, has paid a thumping advance on a book may well venture on a larger first printing number than he would otherwise have contemplated, and may take more trouble over the promotion of the book in question. But by and large it always seemed to me that publishers had to encounter plenty of financial risks in the ordinary course of business, and that it was unfair to saddle them with any more. And I resented the occasional author who tried to push me beyond the figure that I thought I could reasonably go to; and I particularly resented the odd literary agent who persuaded me to name a figure—and then ran off round the corner, told another publisher what I had offered, and came back with a higher bid. This did not, in my experience, happen very often; but I always respected the authors—and the agents—who did not confine their attentions to the single "advance" clause in their agreements. Advances, I thought and still think, should be what their name implies, and not rash speculations. But very few authors will agree with me; and I cannot find it in my heart to blame them. In relation to trouble taken and time expended, the financial rewards of writing a book are, except in rare instances, wretchedly small. If general publishing is, in some ways, a mug's game—so is writing; and if, for one reason or another, a publisher is ass enough to advance more money on a book than it is likely ever to earn, then that is his funeral. If he loses a good author or a good book through sticking to his guns and refusing to cap what he considers to be an unrealistic bid by another publisher, then he must grin and bear it. Time will show whether he has been prudent, or whether, as a business-man engaged in a highly speculative calling, he has failed to be sufficiently daring. I only remember one occasion when a Constable author, on receiving a royalty statement showing that after three years his book had still failed to earn its advance, sent us a cheque for the balance. We were at once surprised, delighted, and a bit embarrassed.

In my own dealings with authors I used to try to treat them as I myself liked being treated by my own publishers. It was not easy, and I often failed. I used sometimes to tell authors that I thought I could understand their feelings because, as a writer, I had been through it all myself. I doubt if this was a good line of approach. I suspect that sometimes they felt that, as a writer, I would be secretly jealous if they had the kind of success that I had been denied. I hope they were wrong. I think they were, because just as I contrived, to far too great an extent, to keep my office life and my home life separate, so I regarded my publishing life and my writing life as two totally different existences. During the whole time I was at Constable's I do not think that I ever, on any single occasion, worked on one of my own books in the office.

If a publisher and an author got badly across one another, I always found that it was better for both parties that the author should take his books elsewhere. Nothing, if he didn't, would go right, and everything would go wrong. One of the really rewarding things about being a publisher was that now and again an easy, friendly and eminently satisfactory publisher-author relationship used to develop. Then, instead of everything going wrong, everything, inevitably, seemed to go right.

I failed dismally in the art of publishing; but I hope that I was reasonably efficient in its practice. I visited Canada, New York and Boston on behalf of the firm; and I always wished that I could have justified the expense of going round the world to meet our agents and representatives to whom I wrote so many letters. And I used to get out of the office as often as I could—which was not very often. Once I went down to the New Forest to visit an author who was a semi-invalid. That night, after he had gone up to bed, his wife shyly told me that she, too, was writing a book. Next morning, when he was driving me to the station, the son of the house told me that he had just finished writing a book. It was the son's book that eventually turned up trumps.

In the last years of his life, when it had got beyond O.K.'s powers, I coped as best I could with George Bernard Shaw. Shaw, by this time, had, to put it mildly, become difficult. For one thing he flatly refused to allow us to put up the published prices of his books. In letter after letter I pointed out to him that he was actually losing money on the sale of every Shaw book that we made on his behalf. I was careful not to add that we ourselves would do better if we were able to take our commission on a more realistic price-range. I should be surprised if this aspect of the case had escaped his notice. He would write back to say that the prices of his books were none of my business; and that in any case he did not want to make any money out of his books. His income was already very large, and the greater part of it was regularly filched by a monstrously rapacious Government. A few days later I would get a letter from him telling me that he did not know where to turn for money. We apparently sold other people's books. Why did we never succeed in selling his?

I remember going down on one occasion to see the old man at Ayot St Lawrence. I suppose that it was about a year before he died. His secretary, Miss Patch, came with me. He greeted me by waving a cutting in my face. It was a bad review of one of our books that had appeared in the *New Statesman* a month or three weeks before. "I do not think very much of the books that Constable's are publishing nowadays," he told me. Maliciously, he must have saved up the cutting with a view to this essay in gamesmanship. I argued with him, as usual, about prices. He was terribly frail. He really did look as if a puff of wind would have blown him over. His thick, ugly, light-coloured cardboardy tweed suit was spotless. The skin stretched tightly over his cheek bones was transparent; and his hair and beard were beautifully white and clean-looking. He was a neat and scrupulously tidy old man. His voice was as strong and as distinctive as ever, and he was in complete control of his wits. When I had stopped trying to argue with him, giving it up as the bad job it evidently was, he became friendly and charming. He recalled his long association with Constable's. He spoke with amused affection of O.K. We had never made a fortune out of his books—he had seen to that; but the prestige of being Shaw's publishers had been considerable. If we had consistently owed him large sums of money over the years, we had also been his debtors in less tangible ways. His housekeeper brought in an excellent tea. "I never take tea," Shaw declared loftily. "Tea is an *unnecessary* meal." I looked round the sitting-room. There were a few interesting things in it but, like the house itself, it was ugly, tasteless and utterly undistinguished. The kind of room and the kind of house that might have belonged to a very conventional insurance broker. After we had said goodbye, and when we were putting on our coats in the hall, Miss Patch, remembering some question she had forgotten to ask, went back into the sitting-room. She came out laughing. "As I expected," she said. "There he was, polishing off all the scones and cakes we didn't eat." Shaw came out, despite our protests, to see us off; and he cross-questioned the chauffeur to make sure that he knew the best way back to London. Shaw always knew all the best ways.

I represented Constable's at his cheerless funeral service, held in one of the chapels at Golders Green crematorium. Surprisingly few people were there. As we straggled in to the chapel, none of us knew where to sit, or indeed what to do. Kneel down? Bow to the altar? But, as I recollect it, there was no altar. Shaw had left instructions that there was to be no religious service. Lady Astor then proceeded to take charge, scuttling round like a trim little sheepdog. The organ played. Very old Sir Sydney Cockerell was helped up into the reading desk, and some sheets of typescript were thrust into his hands. He contrived to hold them upside down, and floundered despairingly. Lady Astor put matters right, and we had a passage from *Pilgrim's Progress* read to us. Casually, as it seemed, Shaw's coffin started to move away. When it had disappeared from view, everything was over. We went out into the rain. There were a few cameramen and reporters. I caught a stinking cold in the head.

One morning in June 1953 I walked the mile and a half across the church fields and by way of Miss Stevens's cherry orchard in order to catch my train to London. Nothing unusual happened until I reached the stretch of road that dips steeply down to the station. Then I suddenly became aware that my right foot had gone stiff and dead. I dragged it along, kicked my shoe as best I could against the outside wall of the booking office, and, by the time I had boarded the train, all seemed to be well again. A few weeks later we went to stay at Schloss Matzen, at Brixlegg, in the Austrian Tirol. I had been to Matzen once before. When I was living at Tennerhof, Ernan and Phyllis Forbes Dennis had been invited to luncheon by its then owner, Mrs Baillie-Grohman; and they had asked if they could bring me. Both the castle and its proprietor had made a great impression on my mind.

Schloss Matzen is built into and on the precipitous end of a long narrow spur which juts out from one of the steep sides of the valley of the River Inn; and from a stone seat in its outer forecourt there is a breathtaking view down this mountain-girt river valley with, in the foreground, two smaller but no less picturesque castles, each perched on its individual crag. Inside,

148

the house is hollow, with all its many rooms ranged round three sides of an open courtyard, and reached by three open-arched, vaulted galleries, one above the other. Mrs Baillie-Grohman was as fascinating and as romantic as the castle she lived in. She was Irish by birth and, having married her cosmo-politan, big-game hunting husband, she had come to Innsbruck on her honeymoon. Driving one day through Brixlegg, she had seen Schloss Matzen towering up above the road. She had there and then fallen in love with the place; and having made in-quiries in the village she had found that it was both derelict and for sale. She had asked her husband if he would buy it for her. He had pooh-poohed the idea of acquiring such an obvious white elephant; whereupon she had sold a pearl necklace and had bought it herself. Thereafter, with a break during the First World War, she had restored and furnished one room each year. There were a great many rooms; but she had lived in, and loved, her castle for a very long time. By 1953, when we went to stay there, the old lady was dead; and the place belonged to one of her grandsons.

One day, soon after our arrival, we all climbed a fairly considerable mountain on the other side of the valley. It was a most successful expedition, but I thought, coming down, that I was walking rather badly. I woke up next morning with agonizing pains in both my legs. I put this down to being out of training; and the pains gradually wore off. Another mountain towered up behind the castle; and I was determined to climb it. No one was particularly keen to come with me. I had chosen a very hot day; and they preferred to bathe. So I set off by myself, taking the post bus to the mountain village from which ascents were usually made. I began to climb at a cracking pace, and before I was through the fir woods my back had begun to ache rather badly. I put this down to some kind of a stitch (though it was an unusual place for stitches); and I thought that it would wear off. It didn't. I got to the top all right, and coming down—I took another route—all went well until I reached the final steep, grassy slope that dropped down to the road that ran up from Brixlegg to the village I had started from. While I was going down this slope crabwise, both my legs suddenly went dead and I fell over. I rolled the rest of the way down, coming to a stop just short of a stream. I tried to get up, found that this was impossible, and dragged myself on to a rock, where I sat wondering rather miserably what was the matter with my legs, and how I was ever going to cross the stream and reach the road. I also thought what a very good thing it had been that this misfortune had not overtaken me at the top of the mountain. I had not seen a soul in the whole course of my climb.

My legs came slowly to life, and after a bit I managed to get across the water. A kind passing motorist gave me a lift to Brixlegg; and I was able to limp back to the castle under my own steam. By the evening I was as right as rain again. A week later we drove over to Kitzbühel to dine in one of the restaurants that had sprung up there since my day. There was a cabaret show of yodellers; and, after that, while I was dancing, my right knee buckled with no warning, and I fell down. This was the second of many tumbles, and the start of a long-drawn-out business of playing a last round of golf, using first one stick and then two, going for a last walk, consulting endless, sympathetic but pessimistic neurologists, going into hospital, taking to elbow crutches, and then to a wheelchair.

One of the consultants I went to urged me to embark on another book. It would, he thought, serve to take my mind off my troubles. So in course of time I wrote a light-hearted novel about a happily married publisher who was unwise enough to bring out a book ostensibly written by a woman with whom he had once been very much in love. Writing *Spring List* served its purpose pretty well; but when I had finished it I reached the conclusion that if I was ever going to write the kind of historical biography that I had always wanted to write, I had better hurry up and find a suitable subject. The future—or rather my future—seemed distinctly uncertain.

Chapter Ten

I WROTE three historical biographies—or, rather, to be more precise, two historical biographies, and one account of a historic quarrel.

The aspiring biographer has first of all to find a subject suitable for the kind of book that he wants to write. There are several courses open to him. At a pinch, he could, I suppose, wade right through all the volumes of the *Dictionary of National Biography*, checking on any "possibles" that he may spot by consulting the London Library Catalogues. Or he can step up his desultory reading in the hope of coming across a reference to someone he has never heard of, but who sounds promising. Or he may get tipped off. A knowledgeable friend may produce a brilliant suggestion; or he may hear about an unpublished diary belonging to an old lady in Taunton; or someone may tell him about a cache of letters or papers in the attic of a country house in Northamptonshire. Inevitably, the tip that sounds the most promising generally turns out the saddest disappointment.

The first of my historical studies was an account of Mary Eleanor Bowes, Countess of Strathmore, and of her grandson, John Bowes. I am pretty sure that I had never heard of this ill-starred lady, and I had certainly never heard of her grandson, until I came across references to both of them in Augustus J. C. Hare's immensely long autobiography, *The Story of My Life*. Hare had a special interest in the Strathmores because his grandmother had been Lady Anne Simpson, sister to the 9th Earl of Strathmore who married Mary Eleanor Bowes in 1767. That Hare (as I found out later) had got Lady Strathmore's story mostly wrong, and that he had gone still further off the rails when he related the confused story of her grandson's parentage, is immaterial, and merely goes to show that history usually gets handed down in any family in a pretty garbled state. What did matter was that his references to Lady Strathmore and John Bowes caught my attention and aroused my interest. It sounded, I thought, a good story; but the chances are that I would have taken no active steps to find out just how good a story it really was if I had not happened to read, a couple of weeks later, the first of two articles in *Country Life* devoted to Gibside, the house and property in County Durham where Mary Eleanor Bowes had been brought up.

Family history—who married who, and the ramifications of this family's connections with that—can easily become an obsession, with Debrett's *Peerage* figuring as an essential source book. I have never been a great "Debrettist"; but I was interested to discover that this eighteenth-century marriage between the only child and heiress of a very rich County Durham landowner and a Scottish peer was the reason why the Earls of Strathmore, of Glamis Castle, still own a great deal of land in the north of England; why, ever since, their family name has been "Bowes-Lyon"; and why Queen Elizabeth, the Queen Mother, spent a part of her childhood at St Paul's, Waldenbury, which was one of the three great houses—Gibside, and Streatlam Castle near Barnard Castle, were the other two—which Mary Eleanor Bowes brought into the family. But what interested me much more were the hints which first Augustus Hare, and then Christopher Hussey, had dropped about this heiress's fantastic life, the improbabilities of which had been repeated, with some marked differences, in the career of her grandson. They were both, I decided, distinctly worth investigating.

The next step, obviously, was to take my coat off and to do some digging. In the general way the most likely places in which to start digging are the British Museum and the London

Library. I struck oil at once. The British Museum possessed a copy of an extremely rare pamphlet,—Lady Strathmore's own *Confessions*, written in 1778 and published, against her wishes, by her scoundrelly second husband, Andrew Robinson Bowes, generally known as "Stoney" Bowes. The London Library produced a less rare but equally useful book, *Lives of Andrew Robinson Bowes Esq., and the Countess of Strathmore*, by Jesse Foot, surgeon, who had been Lady Strathmore's doctor for thirty-three years. The *Confessions* gave a detailed account of Mary Eleanor's childhood, of her engagement and marriage to Lord Strathmore, and of her life up to the time of her second marriage. Foot took the story on from there. I satisfied myself that no one since Foot had devoted a book to the "Unhappy Countess," as Hare always called her. Next to nothing had been written about her grandson, John Bowes. The field was clear, if I wanted to go ahead. And I began to worry madly in case someone else should have lighted on these "possibles" at much the same time as I had. The *Country Life* articles might have put them on the trail.

Stifling this dread, I set about checking the accuracy of the facts that I already possessed. It might turn out that the *Confessions* were largely bogus; and that Foot had invented some or all of his stories. Both books stood up to investigation pretty well. There was no lack of contemporary comment. Lady Strathmore had been "news" from the time she had grown up. She had been the richest heiress of her day, owning thousands of coal-bearing acres in County Durham, Northumberland and Yorkshire. She had married an eligible peer. She had behaved indiscreetly, taking a lover while her ailing husband was still alive. There had been noisy quarrels with her Lyon brother-in-law over her Lyon children. As soon as Lord Strathmore was dead she had married a notorious fortune-hunter after he had pretended that he had been mortally wounded in a fake duel. She had been a gift to the gossip writers of the day; and I found that in its turn I could check much of this lurid information against soberer accounts given in autobiographies and by local historians. Before long I had to make up my mind whether the material I had collected justified embarking on a book.

This is always a difficult decision for a biographer to make. He will already have put in a lot of hard work. It will seem a shame to let it go for nothing. On the other hand he will realize, if he looks his problem squarely in the face, that while some subjects rate a book, others are worth no more than, at the best, a magazine article.

Having sat on the fence for a while, I came down on the side of trying to write Mary Eleanor's life story largely because I was puzzled and intrigued by the problem of what she had really been like. If she had, in fact, been no more than a silly, empty-headed, irresponsible, over-sexed woman with a deplorable taste in men, no moral sense, a fondness for the bottle and far more money than was good for her, she clearly would not have been worth bothering about. In one sense she had been all these things; but I had gradually come to the conclusion that she had possessed other and more attractive qualities. Until she had been spoilt and corrupted by an incompatible first marriage, by an unscrupulous lover, and by the awful and sadistic "Stoney" Bowes, she had been, I believed—indeed I was certain—potentially a woman of real talent, considerable distinction, great charm and genuine sensibility—and, to a certain rather pathetic extent, she had retained vestiges of these qualities even after she had been dragged through acres of unspeakably filthy eighteenth-century mud. I was haunted by the conception of the person she might have been if she had had less money and if she had married someone whom she had loved and respected; and I dare say that by this time I had, up to a point, fallen half in love with her myself. This is at once a helpful and a dangerous situation for a biographer to find himself in. I was finally confirmed in my decision by the visit I paid to Gibside.

Romantic ruins have always attracted me strongly. Gibside,

when I went to see it, proved to be one of the most romantic, as well as one of the most thoroughly ruined, ruins that I had ever encountered. The winding drive, designed by Mary Eleanor's father to surprise and delight visitors to his house—it ran through hanging beech woods and passed, in succession, a banqueting house in the Gothic taste, a fantasticated bathing pavilion, an immensely tall stone column topped by the figure of Liberty, and a classical stable block—had become little more than a rough mossy trackway. All the beeches had been felled; and the "eye-catching" follies had degenerated into tottering, bramble-infested wrecks. The great house itself was a roofless, empty shell; and the mile-long avenue that fronted it, running from the column of Liberty to the exquisite little mausoleum chapel designed by Paine, had merged with the rough grass of the park. The view from the terrace was marred by slag heaps and coal workings. But I was fascinated by this vast derelict demesne—partly, I suppose, because I had spent long hours trying to reconstruct its layout from the information contained in the *Country Life* articles, and it was exciting to discover, on the actual ground, where my sketch maps had gone wrong; and partly because this had been the one place, and possibly the one thing, that Mary Eleanor had loved with a genuine and lifelong passion. Gibside made the strongest possible impression on my mind.

Coming down to earth, in the course of this visit I had a remarkable stroke of good fortune. Once Mary Eleanor had succeeded in escaping from her second husband, she had become embroiled in a whole series of complicated Chancery actions designed to recover what was left of the Bowes fortune. Even with the help of a friend who is a Chancery Queen's Counsel I had been unable to make head or tail of these protracted legal proceedings. The agent for the Gibside property had taken a whole day off to drive me round in his Land-Rover; and when I was saying goodbye to him he mentioned casually that in a shooting-lodge on the Yorkshire moors, which also belonged to Lord Strathmore, he had recently noticed a mass of old legal-looking documents stuffed away in a cupboard. Would they, he wondered, be of any use to me? I said that I should most certainly like to see them; and a few weeks later this kind man turned up in Orange Street with a Gladstone bag stuffed with papers. One of them was the brief prepared for Counsel in the very last Chancery action of all; and it was prefaced by a full summary of all the earlier proceedings so succinct and clear that even I could understand it. One of the main stumbling blocks to my progress had been removed.

To the detriment of the symmetry of the book, I had decided very early on not to stop at Lady Strathmore's death, but to continue the story so as to cover the lives of her eldest son, John, Earl of Strathmore, and of his only son, John Bowes.

John Bowes had attracted me because he had been at once so lucky and so unlucky, so successful and so unsuccessful. He was born out of wedlock. His father was the 10th Earl and his mother, Mary Milner, a housemaid. When his birth was registered, his name had been put down as John Bowes Milner. Then his father, who was devoted to the boy, decreed that he should be known as John Bowes; and as John Bowes he had been sent to school. On his death-bed Lord Strathmore had married Mary Milner; and the boy's headmaster had been informed that his pupil should now be addressed as Lord Glamis. Twenty-four hours later these instructions had been changed. Lord Glamis had become the 11th Earl of Strathmore. Finally, as the result of a ruling by the Committee of Privileges on a petition presented by the boy's Lyon uncle, he had had to revert to being plain John Bowes again. But, under the terms of his father's will, he had inherited all the coal-bearing properties in the north of England. Though he had had no title he had been fabulously rich.

He was elected to Parliament, he won the Derby no less than four times and, with his wife, he amassed one of the greatest of all the great nineteenth-century collections of old master paintings, furniture and china. He was bored by the House of Commons, he seldom if ever attended a race meeting, and he would gladly have exchanged every art treasure he possessed for a son and heir. He was extremely active, at one time, in the Newcastle and Durham coal and shipping trades, but as he preferred living in his house in Paris to living at Streatlam Castle he had to conduct his business affairs at long range. He married a French actress and planned to install his treasures in a great museum to be erected just outside Calais. Alarmed by the political unrest in France, he ordered the monstrous château, designed by Pellechet, to be built at Barnard Castle. He was probably happiest when he owned and managed a theatre in Paris. Thackeray, who had been at Cambridge with him, found him a bore; and he contrived, right at the end of his life, to lose most of his money.

I spent several happy days at the Bowes Museum, going through packet after packet of the letters written from Paris by its founder to his agent and his solicitor. John Bowes was, as I am now prepared to admit, an extraneous addition which upset the shape of my book: but I had great fun trying to understand the workings of the Northumberland and County Durham coal trade; and how his Derby winners had been bred. And I would not for the world have missed reading the acrimonious correspondence which he had conducted with the Company which proposed to bring the railway to Barnard Castle, passing over his land well to the south of Streatlam Castle. "I do not consider that the railway would be an advantage to me personally," Mr Bowes wrote, "but on the contrary, passing where it does, and breaking in on our privacy, I consider it a nuisance." Sensibly, however, he appreciated that the line would be of benefit to Barnard Castle, and he was prepared to permit this outrage—on the one condition that he should be provided with a private railway station of his very own. The question of the station itself, and of its staffing, worried him. "It will be necessary," he wrote to his solicitor, "for me to have someone always living there, as at a lodge. . . . The Company had better agree to build a cottage, and they can let it to some respectable person, who will attend to the signalling, receiving the letter bags, etc."

My next book was a Life of James Radcliffe, 3rd Earl of Derwentwater. I appeared to have a predilection for earls. It was, I am sorry to say, a failure; and as such can be passed over quickly. Up to the time that I was seven years old we had lived with my grandmother, my mother's mother, at Meopham; and my grandmother had been a Grey of Milfield, in Northumberland. More importantly, though no Grey of Milfield would ever have agreed that anything could be more important than being a Grey of Milfield, her uncle had been the noted agriculturalist, John Grey of Dilston—and Dilston had been the Northumbrian seat of the Radcliffes, Earls of Derwentwater. So I had been brought up on the story of the gentle and unhappy young man who, if only his wife had left him alone, would have lived happily at home, would have forgotten that he was Charles II's grandson, and would never have led the disastrous Northumbrian Jacobite Rising in 1715. I had sometimes wondered, after I had grown up, how much of the Derwentwater legend was true, and how much of it was nonsense; but I should probably have contented myself with mild speculations if a cousin of my wife's had not been the owner of Capheaton Hall, midway between Newcastle upon Tyne and Carter Bar; and if this same cousin had not one day told me that among the family papers at Capheaton there were all the letters written by James Derwentwater to his cousin and confidante, the Lady Swinburne of the day, before the Rising, during the brief campaign that ended at Preston, and while he was held prisoner in the Tower of London awaiting execution. These letters, I knew, had been seen by only one historian, the Rev. John Hodgson, who had used brief extracts from them in his *History of Northumberland*, published in 1827. "Why," she had said, "don't you use them as the basis for a new Life of Lord D.?"

Virtually unseen and unpublished material attracts historical biographers in much the same way as catmint is said to attract cats. More unwanted historical studies have been written on the strength of uninteresting unpublished material than for any other single reason. I have no reason to believe that Lord Derwentwater's letters to Lady Swinburne would have turned out to be uninteresting. On the contrary, the tantalizing extracts that Hodgson printed suggest strongly that Lord Derwentwater was a good letter-writer; and that these letters would have been enormously helpful to anyone who wanted to understand what kind of a young man James Derwentwater had really been. The fact is that I have never, to this day, set eyes on a single one of them.

This was not a case of a member of a family promising help and support, and then suddenly withdrawing it—a very real menace that confronts all historical biographers. Everyone concerned was convinced that the letters were in one of six great coffers or trunks that stood in the long upstairs library at Capheaton. In due course each of these coffers was opened. The blood-stained shirt that Lord Derwentwater had worn on the scaffold was there all right; and so were a few other Derwentwater relics—but there was no trace of the letters. What had probably happened to them, and the fruitless efforts that I made to discover their present whereabouts, is a long, sad story. It is sufficient to say that I do not know, to this day, who owns them, or where they are.

With the principal *raison d'être* of the book removed, I should by rights have abandoned the project. There had already been three Lives of Lord Derwentwater, and mine would make a redundant and probably unnecessary fourth. But I fell into the old, familiar trap. I had already done a great deal of work on my subject. I had become fascinated by the story of the

Radcliffes in the seventeenth century who, Roman Catholic recusants to a man, had succeeded in finishing the century richer than they had been at its start. I had succeeded, to my own satisfaction, in establishing that much of the "Derwentwater Legend" was bosh. I had acquired a deep affection for the 3rd Earl. And, most unwisely, I had become interested in the Derwentwater Claimant, an eccentric woman who, in the 1860s, had announced that she was the rightful owner of the Derwentwater estates, which had reverted to the Crown on the death, as a minor, of the 3rd Earl's only son.

So, without the letters, I went ahead and completed my book. It taught me a good deal of history and, I hope, a salutary lesson.

I stumbled on my third subject by pure and absolute chance. After my father's death, going through a mass of papers that had belonged to my grandfather, I came across a pamphlet entitled *Cathedral Trusts and their Fulfilment*. Its author was the Rev. Robert Whiston, and it had been published in 1849. I believe that I was vaguely aware that a Mr Whiston had been headmaster of the Rochester Cathedral Grammar School in the nineteenth century; and that he had had a tremendous row with the Dean and Chapter of Rochester over money. Further than that I could not have gone; and I would almost certainly have thrown this pamphlet into the wastepaper basket—Victorian clergymen were prolific and usually pretty dull pamphleteers—but for one thing. Scrawled on its title-page was the name "George Essell"; and George Essell, I recalled, had been the Chapter Clerk at Rochester when my grandfather had first gone to the office on College Green. This association-link was just sufficiently strong to induce me to take a second look at this booklet; and I at once saw that its former owner had not only sidelined and underlined passage after passage in the text, but had also written in the margins such comments as "This is NOT so"; "Demonstrably false": and, more mildly, "NOT true". I observed, too, that Mr Essell's own name occurred pretty frequently and, intrigued, I read the pamphlet through. Apart from the fact that it had evidently been written by a scholar in a towering rage, a consideration that had occasionally upset the balance and organization of the narrative, *Cathedral Trusts* told a fascinating story extremely well. If only the half of its allegations were true, Mr Whiston, as it seemed to me, had an overwhelming case; and the Deans and Chapters not only of Rochester but of all the other Cathedrals refounded by Henry VIII must, for hundreds of years, have been feathering their own nests at the expense of their Cathedral Grammar Boys and their Exhibitioners at Oxford and Cambridge.

The Rev. Robert Whiston might, I decided, be worth looking into; and it was at this point that I remembered, or thought that I remembered, that he had been mentioned in Anthony Trollope's *The Warden*. I hunted up a copy of the first of the Barsetshire novels, and found that I had been right. Archdeacon Grantly "had written letters to the public press on the subject of the turbulent Dr Whiston which, as his admirers think, must well nigh set the question at rest"; and the Archdeacon, at Dr Harding's party, had been overheard bombasting about "the damnable business of Mr Whiston." From Michael Sadleir's *Trollope: A Commentary* I discovered that the story of *The Warden* had been conceived in May or June 1851, when the Rochester dispute had been at its height, and when it had been attracting a great deal of notice in the newspapers; and I also found that when Trollope had later submitted his manuscript to Longmans, their Reader had begun his report: "This story takes its rise from the recent exposure of the abuses that have crept into Cathedral and Hospital Trusts."

Further investigations disclosed that Trollope had indeed obtained the material for his plot from the published reports of two clerical scandals—the Whiston dispute at Rochester, and the case of the Hospital of St Cross at Winchester; and in Trollope's own autobiography I found one other interesting fact. When he wrote *The Warden* he had never lived in a Cathedral city, he had no first-hand knowledge of the ways of a close, and no archdeacon had as yet crossed his path. He had been guided solely by his novelist's instinct and by these published reports. If, it occurred to me, I could discover what the Dean and the other members of the Chapter at Rochester, and their Visitor, the Bishop, had really been like in 1848, and how they had actually behaved in the course of the Whiston dispute, I would be in a position to judge how accurate, or how inaccurate, Trollope's instinct had been. As an ardent Trollopian this prospect excited me.

Mr Whiston, I found, had been ignored by the editors of *The Dictionary of National Biography*. I came on a few references to him in Histories of Rochester—but they did not get me much further. Then, in desperation, I rang up the present Chapter Clerk. "This," I said, "is a pretty long shot, but have you by any chance still got in the office any of the papers connected with the Whiston dispute?" He asked me what the Whiston dispute had been about, and when it had taken place; and I told him. He sounded dubious, but said that he would go and have a look in the Chapter strong-room. Half an hour later he was back on the telephone. If, he told me, I cared to send a three-ton lorry in to Rochester I could have what appeared at first sight to be every single document and every single letter connected with the case.

This material duly arrived in six huge sacks. My wife was not best pleased. The sacks blocked up my room, and the papers they contained were dirty and dusty. This dirt and dust spread slowly through the entire house. Months passed before I had sorted through the last sack; and then I began the lengthy job of extracting from these original documents the story of the dispute that had begun with a letter written on 9 February 1848, and that ended at a Chapter Meeting held on 1 January 1853.

Few amateur historians can ever have been presented with a

more complete documentation. Every scrap of paper connected with the Chapter's side of the dispute had been scrupulously kept. Even notes scribbled by the Canons at Chapter meetings and handed to their Clerk had been preserved. The Counsels' briefs, some of them annotated by Roundell Palmer in his own illegible handwriting, I found especially interesting; and the transcripts of the shorthand writers' notes of the various court hearings ran to thousands of folio pages, all written in a copper-plate hand.

I thoroughly enjoyed working on the Whiston Matter, which was how the Chapter members always referred to the dispute. Both the story itself and the people involved in it seemed to me to become progressively more and more interesting. When I began, my sympathies were entirely with Mr Whiston, whom I regarded as a fearless reformer pitting his puny strength against entrenched privilege in the shape of cathedral dignitaries bloated with riches dishonestly filched from the deserving poor. By the time I had finished, while I retained a sincere admiration for the Headmaster's energy, courage in adversity, skill as a disputant, and grasp of the basic principles of publicity, I had come to feel pretty sorry for the Dean and Canons of Rochester, badly and stupidly as they had behaved, and careless as they had been in carrying out many of the obligations laid down in their Statutes. In Mr Whiston they had been up against a truly terrible opponent—relentless, angry, untiring, unscrupulous and absolutely certain that he was right. For the Lord Bishop of Rochester, Dr George Murray, and for the Chapter Clerk, Mr George Essell, I had no sympathy at all. They, in my view, were the villains of the piece.

I was able to visit the actual scenes of the conflict; and I spent a long afternoon in the chapter-room where Mr Whiston had so often confronted his opponents. It had changed very little; and in this long quiet room overlooking the Deanery garden, where Dean Hole later grew his celebrated roses, I felt extraordinarily close to the long-dead characters with whom I had been spending so much of my spare time. In the course of this same afternoon I was caught out, as many a better historian had been caught out before me.

Glancing along the chapter-room shelves I noticed a History of Rochester that was new to me. I took it down, turned up "Whiston" in its index, and found a reference to a piece entitled *The History of a Certain Grammar School*, contributed anonymously by Charles Dickens to *Household Words*, the magazine that he had edited. I had been surprised that Dickens had apparently refrained from entering the Whiston fray; and had put it down to a snobbish fear on his part of annoying his neighbours, the Dean and Canons. I had evidently misjudged him. I got the appropriate bound volume of *Household Words* out of the London Library, and read the piece. It was an entertainingly satirical account of the dispute and, though it named no names, it came down strongly on the Headmaster's side. I am no Dickens expert; but it read like Dickens, and the Rochester historian had stated categorically that Dickens had written it. I said as much in my own book. Soon after *The Whiston Matter* had been published I was severely rapped over the knuckles. The piece in question, I was told, had not been written by Charles Dickens —a fact that I could have discovered for myself if I had taken the trouble to make inquiries in the right quarter. This reproof was deserved.

I was haunted, while I was writing this book, by a lost opportunity. Despite the documentation at my disposal, I found it hard to discover what kind of a man Mr Whiston had really been. Only one member of his family, a cousin who had never known him, was still living. A few very old people in Rochester could just remember the headmaster as an alarming old man with a long white beard. I felt, after reading dozens and dozens of his letters, that I had a pretty good idea of what he had been like— but I could not be certain that I was right. And yet if I had chanced to mention Mr Whiston's name in the course of any of those innumerable visits that I had paid to Cobhambury I should have been given a vivid and enlightening character-sketch, for my grandfather, who lived to be ninety-six, had entered the Cathedral Grammar School in 1848, the very year in which the dispute had started; and Mr Whiston had been his headmaster from the start to the finish of his school career.

I had difficulty, too, in assessing the characters of Mr Whiston's opponents for, with the exception of Dr Hawkins, Provost of Oriel College, Oxford, none of the Rochester Canons had been in any way famous or well known. It was a certain Canon John Griffith, the Headmaster's bitterest enemy, about whom I could discover least, and about whom I should have liked to have known most. Why, I wondered again and again, had he been so bitter, and why had he been filled with such an over-whelming sense of his own importance? I found a possible answer to these questions after my book had been published. It was reviewed most generously by an eminent Oxford professor who, nevertheless, took me to task for telling my readers so little about this important character; and he rubbed salt in my wounds by recounting a Griffith anecdote which I should dearly have liked to have found for myself before the book went to press. I wrote and asked him about its provenance; and he replied that he had discovered it in the *Record of Old West-minsters*.

I could not have known, when I used to go to Cobhambury, that I would one day write a book about Mr Whiston. I had known perfectly well, while I was writing *The Whiston Matter*, that Dr Griffith had been a scholar of Westminster School, for on several occasions the Headmaster had upbraided him for having himself in the past accepted a more generous bounty than he was willing to extend to the Rochester scholars. It had been abominably careless of me not to have looked him up in the Register of his old school. I repaired this omission, locking the stable door after the horse had been stolen; and I found that the anecdote, when followed up, was even more signifi-cant than had appeared at first sight. I discovered for the first time that Dr Griffith had been a very rich man, which probably accounted for his arrogance; and that when he was subsequently defrauded by a dishonest private bank, he, alone among the creditors, had insisted on bringing a criminal charge against the fraudulent bankers. Evidently, he was a man with a vindictive streak in his make-up.

*   *   *

None of these people whom I wrote about was straightforwardly good or straightforwardly bad. I would offer any odds that if and when the Derwentwater-Swinburne correspondence ever turns up, the accepted version of James Derwentwater's character will have to be drastically revised. I have an uneasy feeling that all his biographers, myself included, have got him wrong. I think and hope that I was nearer the mark in my assessments of Lady Strathmore and of Mr Whiston.

Chapter Eleven

I HAVE overshot two events of great importance to Constable's—O.K.'s retirement, and Michael Sadleir's illness and death.

O.K. did not, in the event, die in harness. He suddenly announced, in December 1953, that he was going to retire. In part this decision was dictated by age and failing health; but I am afraid that he also felt that he was no longer of any great use to the firm, and that he was no longer wanted. This is a horrible situation which, in the end, faces most publishers. For a time the waning star can exist fairly happily on the strength of his position as chairman, and on the prestige of his past achievements. He is kept reasonably busy (as busy, probably, as he wants to be) by his old contacts. But since he either has not wanted to take on any new authors or, in effect, has not been allowed to, and as his old commitments dwindle—writers die or stop writing, old publishing friends both here and in America disappear, and the familiar heads of printing and binding works are replaced by younger men—he finds himself with progressively less and less to do, and the law of diminishing effort leading to diminishing energy begins to operate. The less he has to do, the less he finds himself able to do. In any community the drone is resented. He may be loved or respected; but, secretly or openly, he is resented all the same. And well he knows it. O.K. must have been aware of a situation of this kind for long enough. It had been terribly hard not to get impatient with him. The "little talks" had taken up such a lot of my time when I had had so little time to spare—and yet they had been,

167

I suspect, one of the Old Gentleman's great pleasures. He had become increasingly slow and bumbling at meetings; and he could be maddeningly obstinate, though quite often he had been all too right when he had opposed something that the rest of us had been bent on doing. Deep down Michael, I know, was as devoted as ever to the old man, and so was Martha, and so was I. But Michael could, on occasions, be tactless; and I was far too often far too impatient. But he was spared the worst, the very worst, indignity that can befall a publisher on the wane.

In Orange Street—and I cannot speak for other publishing houses—the decision to publish or to reject any given book was always taken, at least in theory, collectively by the people sitting round the Boardroom table at our Wednesday afternoon manuscript meetings. And we had one golden and scrupulously observed rule—no subsequent recriminations. If a book we had taken flopped, no one was permitted to say afterwards, "Well, it was you who was so anxious that we should accept it; and, if you remember, I said at the time that I thought it was no good." If a book which we had rejected did well on someone else's list, no one was allowed to say, "Well, as you may recall, I was always in favour of our taking it." The decision, either way, had been a collective decision; the responsibility was a collective responsibility. This was a good rule.

In practice, of course, decisions to accept or reject a manuscript involved a good deal of give and take. One member of the Board might press the claims of a certain manuscript and, if a colleague was against it, he would try to persuade him that his doubts were unfounded. Usually, unless his objections were extremely strong, the doubter would give way. For one thing he would realize that if someone else felt so strongly there must be something "to" the book in question; for another, he was aware that their positions might be reversed on a subsequent Wednesday. In all the time I was at Constable's I never remember any occasion when an issue in dispute had to be settled by a

168

vote taken round the table. We had some tremendous wrangles over manuscripts, but we always managed to reach an amicable agreement in the end. Necessarily, however, there were always books on the list that any one of the directors regarded as "his" books, others that he liked and thoroughly approved of, others that he was indifferent about, and a few that he actively disliked but which, for the sake of the firm, he genuinely hoped might do better than he thought they deserved. But, for the waning star, the time inevitably came when there were precious few books that he could think of as "his"; and when, probably, there were a good many titles on the list that he disliked or despised, but which he had felt powerless, or unwilling, to block. No one, he may have feared, listened any more to a word he said. His taste was probably considered hopelessly old-fashioned. It was only fair to give the younger generation its head, and to let his colleagues learn the hard way. Then—and this is what I think of as a publisher's last indignity—he might reach a point where he *wanted* these books that he disliked so much to do badly when they came out, so that he could have the satisfaction of at least thinking, "I told you so."

I am convinced that O.K. never once harboured, or could ever have harboured, a "death wish" of this kind for any Constable book. I know that he thought very little of some of the books that we took; and he was quite often proved right. But they carried the Constable imprint; and he was too deeply committed, and far too devoted, to Constable's best interests ever to wish any of them anything but well.

He retired with a minimum of fuss. One day he was in his office as usual, an apparently immovable feature in the Orange Street landscape. The next he just was not there; and in the callous order of things I moved into his room. He never came back to see us. I do not think that he could have borne to. He often used to ring me up, and he continued to take a passionate interest in everything we were doing, and in how things were going. From a combination of wretched circumstances, one of

169

which was a lack of other interests, his retirement was, I am afraid, an unhappy one. He had left it too late; and in any case publishing, and Constable's, had been almost his whole life. But, right up to the day of his death, his astonishing memory never deserted him. I could ask him on the telephone about a book that Constable's had published in, say, 1908. He would not only remember all about the book and its author, he would also be able to recall, in some detail, the terms of its agreement. He was a great publisher of the old school—and a pretty good school that was.

Michael's tragic illness, and his death at the end of 1957, were sorry blows for Constable's. They removed, far too soon, a brilliant, slightly unpredictable, but enormously distinguished figure from the bridge; and upset what I have called the natural law of publishing succession. Even if I had not been, by this time, very badly crippled, I was ill-situated to succeed him. There should have been a period during which he could have gradually handed over to me his authors and his responsibilities. Even if that had happened it is very doubtful if I could ever have filled his place adequately. Suddenly called on to try, when I was incapable, physically, of getting about to see the people that I ought to have seen, and when I could not even climb the stairs to see my colleagues and my staff in their own offices, it was doubly hard to step into his shoes.

By rights, after it was clear that I would never be able to walk again, I should have retired. That I did not do so was due to a number of reasons, some of them entirely selfish. I *could* still go on in a half-cock fashion, and when I had been obliged to give up a great many activities, I was inclined to cling to any that were still just possible. Everyone at the office was extraordinarily kind, and made things as easy as possible for me. It surprised me to discover how unexpectedly thoughtful people could be. There were certain things that I wanted to finish, and others that I wanted to start, before I handed over. And I thought that it would be useful, at least for a time, to retain a link between the old régime and the new régime that would, in some combination in which Michael's surviving son, Richard, would play an essential part, eventually take over.

By the second half of the 1950s our publishing "honeymoon" had ended, and the main problem facing a medium to small publishing house was the problem of survival. A number of the smaller firms had either been bought up by one of the big "publishing empires," or had sunk without much trace. We had missed our chance, directly after the war, of entering the remunerative, but highly competitive, educational text-book field. We were general publishers, with a useful list of advanced scientific and technical books. Did it really matter, except to ourselves, to our individual and corporate prides, to our authors, and to our old employees, whether we survived or not? Was there, I sometimes used to wonder, a place in the publishing economy for smallish independent firms like ours?

With their much larger sales forces, their grandiose publicity resources, their overseas branches and, above all, their incomparably greater reserves of capital, the "big boys" in publishing, as it seemed to me, were better fitted than the "small boys" to handle the big, sensational book. But, in saying that, I am not for one single moment suggesting that a small publisher, if a potential big seller comes his way, should not grasp it with both hands. Of course he should. While I was at Constable's we were lucky enough to bring out several very large sellers. We sold as many copies of them, I suspect, as anyone else would have done; we made a nice lot of money for their authors and for ourselves; and, since nothing in publishing succeeds like success, they did us the world of good. It has sometimes been argued that a best-seller can ruin a small publisher. This, with due respect, seems to me to be nonsense—so long as the small publisher keeps his head. What I did strongly feel, and what I still strongly feel, is that the medium-sized or small publisher should be wary of attempting to ape the ways of the giants. The big seller should, preferably, come to him without his having to bid for it at what amounts to an informal auction held by a literary agent determined to get the biggest possible advance for his client. As a general rule, he would be rash to risk a great deal of money in order to buy the British rights in a huge American novel that has not yet been written. And he would probably be wise to leave the essentially topical book, which will require a big pre-publication build-up, to someone else. But in a great many ways the small publisher can, and does, score over the big battalions.

The small publisher cannot afford to do less than his best for every single book on his list. It is possible, in a big firm, for a manuscript to be accepted, and for it to enter the sausage machine, and come out at the other end, without anyone with much responsibility ever taking an individual or special interest in it. That is, virtually, an impossibility in a smaller firm. Again, big firms tend, sometimes, to concentrate unduly on their big books. These giants rank as "big business"; and they may believe that only big books are "big business." Less obviously important books often require, and may sometimes deserve, just as much care and attention.

The medium-sized and small publisher, as I see it, is valuable in a direct ratio to the kind of books he brings out. Here, too, in my view, the small publisher will be failing in his proper mission in publishing life if he simply tries to ape his larger rivals. If one of the big boys has done well with a book about the Royal Family, the small publisher will probably be ill-advised to scratch round and try to put another book about the Royal Family together. If someone else's big cookery book has been a smashing success, it would generally be a mistake for him to try to find someone to write a still bigger cookery book. If a big publisher has hired the Albert Hall for a pre-publication party, it is unnecessary for his humbler rival to start making inquiries about how much it would cost to take Olympia for the evening.

The list of a small publishing house can and should reflect the tastes and interests of its partners or directors to an extent that is

172

not always possible in the case of larger enterprises. Year in, year out, there should be an idiosyncratic flavour about the books that come out under a small publishers imprint—they should, recognizably, be the kind of books, within the widest possible terms of reference, that his firm is known for; and he should be more, rather than less, willing than his larger competitors to try his luck with new writers. It would be nice to think that the author of an out of the ordinary first book, or a literary agent who has got hold of a manuscript which he considers "difficult" but potentially promising, might reasonably feel that it would be a better idea to entrust it to a good small publishing house than to a good large one.

I do not mean to suggest that a small publisher should publish only books that are strongly to his own taste—blandly ignoring the issue as to whether they will also be to the taste of the reading public. Nor do I mean to suggest that his list ought to be wholly or mainly "experimental". Ideally, his taste in books should coincide with the taste of at least a substantial section of book-buyers and book-borrowers; and he will be well-advised to father some titles which may not in any way interest or excite him—provided that they are good books in their own right, and that he and his colleagues think that they are good bets. The main thing is to avoid publishing a book which is recognized in the house as being shoddy or meretricious or second-rate, but which somebody optimistically believes will be a seller. Nine out of ten times it won't be. If he consistently sets his sights reasonably high, now and again, with any luck, the small publisher will find himself with a book that sells very well indeed.

Unless a small publisher can rely on a solid back list—which in its turn derives from a past policy of publishing worthwhile books—or on a list of reliable titles in a specialized field, the occasional best-seller may be the only thing that will keep him afloat. Appropriately, the great majority of writers are in much the same boat. Most authors go on writing books, in return for pitifully small financial rewards, either because they enjoy

173

writing and would be miserable if they stopped, or because they have a lively hope that one day they will strike it lucky. Without this shared hope there would be precious few publishers, and precious few authors.

From time to time the small publisher must expect to get stung. By a combination of hard work and good fortune he will have succeeded in establishing a writer's reputation and then, just when he is congratulating himself on being in secure possession of a desirable "property," his treasured author may be lured away from him to lusher fields. I cannot recall a single instance of a publisher, so long as he remained solvent, deliberately diddling or defrauding an author. But publishers, in my experience, are not always quite as scrupulous in their dealings with one another.

So much for theory. In practice the small publisher is constantly subjected to pressures that push him in the direction of doing all kinds of things that he should not do. Take the matter of book production. Here again he may well have the inside edge on the big publisher. Publishers in a big way of business can afford to employ typographical experts; but success in book production does not always stem from having experts on the staff. It more often comes from the exercise of taste, and from taking infinite pains. But a great many circumstances may conspire to persuade the small publisher to let things pass that should never be allowed to pass. It may be a question of scrapping a set of illustration blocks which are unsatisfactory—but not quite bad enough to warrant a credit from the blockmaker. New blocks will cost quite a lot of money; and it may be plausibly argued that no one outside the house will notice the difference. Or it may be a question of time. The print in a book planned for publication in early November has offset. By rights, the printer should be made to do the job again, but that would mean that the book would have to be postponed until the spring. With a small list, this may appear, at the time, to be a major disaster. Better, perhaps, to let it go?

174

Then there is the much bigger question of the size of his list. The small publisher will be told by his accountants that he must not only strive to keep his annual turnover up, he must contrive each year to push it higher. Only in this way can he hope to meet his constantly rising overheads. At first sight, one of the easiest ways of accomplishing this difficult feat is to publish more books.

There is a comforting theory, to which I never subscribed, that the more books a firm publishes in any one year, the more likely is it that a winner will turn up. It is never particularly hard to find books to publish. The difficulty is to find the right books. Other things being equal, I often used to think that the medium-sized publisher might be well-advised to demote himself to the status of a small publisher; and that the small publisher might, with advantage, become smaller still. But of course other things never *are* equal. Accountants are perfectly right; and it is essential to have a considerable amount of money coming in from sales all the time in order to be in a position to afford a proper office staff and an adequate force of travellers. It is always possible to share travellers with another firm, and to farm out the chores of accounting, packing and despatching to a central agency. But this, in a way, is a bit like living in a service flat. It saves trouble, but it can be an expensive way of life; and perhaps it is more satisfactory, since mistakes have to be made, to make one's own. Probably, when all is said and done, the best course for the medium-sized or small publisher to pursue is to plug along, doing his damnedest to push his turnover up each year without sacrificing either the quality of the content, or the quality of the production, of the books that he brings out. If he does that he is, in my view, performing a useful publishing function.

We plugged along more or less like this through the late 1950s. We provided travelling, accounting, packing and despatching services for a new firm that specialized in art books, and for a University Press which started up in 1950. The Art

Book firm outgrew us; the University Press remains a staunch friend and ally. I was instrumental in starting one new departure at Orange Street—a list of children's books. And I like to think that thanks to Grace Hogarth's editorial flair, taste, knowledge and persistence this was about the best thing I ever did for the firm.

At 4.30 p.m. on Wednesday 18 April 1962, I was sitting in my car in the main street of Kenmare, drinking a cup of tea. My wife had fetched it for me from a nearby café. In the course of the afternoon we had driven along the north side of Bantry Bay. The narrow winding road had commanded a changing prospect of mountains and of water. Sometimes there had been more mountains in sight than water, and sometimes it had been the other way round. We had encountered remarkably few fellow motorists, but we had shared the road with a great many hobbled horses and donkeys, grazing peacefully on the verges; pigs going about their own business; black-faced sheep that found the road a nice warm place to lie on; hens, ducks and geese; small boys and girls in nominal charge of cows and bullocks; old ladies with shawls over their heads; and a wide variety of horse-drawn vehicles. Spring had come with a rush, and everything was shining. I had liked the road best when it had run close to the Bay where, in the little inlet harbours, boats were being got ready for the summer. On the landward side, between the road and the line of mountains, there had been small, very green meadows, spangled with daisies and dandelions; and scattered white farmsteads surrounded by trees that were just coming into leaf. There had been giant primroses on the grassy road banks; periwinkles in flower in the miles of fuchsia hedges that still looked like faggots of dead sticks; and everywhere holly trees and masses of gorse in full bloom. Then we had doubled back, and had crossed the Caha Mountains by the Healy Pass. And so we had come, at tea time, to Kenmare.

176

At 4.30 p.m. on this very day a meeting, as I knew, had been called in the Boardroom at 10 Orange Street to consider, and accept, my formal resignation from the firm. Back in London, as I drank my tea and observed the quiet tempo of life in Kenmare High Street, the last grain of sand was trickling out of my publishing hour-glass. A new and, as I sincerely hoped, a successful and distinguished era in Constable's continuing life would begin—but I would not be there to share in it.

Chapter Twelve

I NEVER get tired of Brickhole Lane, which is fortunate, because when I am at home at Cobham, and provided that the weather and the going are reasonably good, I wobble and lurch down it in my electric tricycle two or three times a week. When I first got this machine I was under the impression that its "marque" name was "Argosy." To its driver, this romantic appellation, or something very like it, appears, written upside down, on the base of its tiller. It was rather a let-down when I discovered that the name was actually "Argson." For all that it is a very good and serviceable electric tricycle, resembling an old-fashioned bath-chair; and in it I am able to proceed slowly and silently along the roads of the parish and, except when the ground is too wet, I can also negotiate grassy lanes, footpaths if they are wide enough, rides through the woods if they are not too deeply rutted, and, under especially favourable conditions, grass fields, orchards and, in the autumn, stubbles.

An electric tricycle has certain advantages over a motor-car. When driving it, it is possible to look at the passing scene without any great danger of running off the road. Stopping to pass the time of day with someone or to investigate some interesting phenomenon does not result in a traffic block. And there is no bedevilling compulsion to pass other slower vehicles. There are no slower vehicles. Pedestrians, somewhat mystified by a ghostly rhythmic whirring at their heels, are the only fellow road-users whom I ever overtake. Even across country it has its points. In theory, going for a walk should be the best possible way of seeing the countryside. But I used to find, in practice, that it seldom worked out that way. I would set off for a solitary walk determined to take particular note of, say, woods, or the pattern of fields, or the system of roads, lanes and paths. But what with one thing and another—a dog that had to be shouted at and made to stay to heel, short cuts that proved to be mistakes, the physical exertion of walking and, above all, trains of extraneous and intruding thoughts—I nearly always returned home not much wiser than I had been when I set out. There is something about the slow, gliding motion of an electric tricycle that positively encourages observation, thought, and a reasonably connected line of speculation.

Brickhole Lane runs from the back of my house down a long slope to the foot of a wooded ridge. It is a grass-grown lane which now serves as a farm access road; but it used to be an integral part of the road system of the parish, connecting the village with the main London to Dover highway. For some reason, when all the roads and lanes were taken over by the County Council, Brickhole Lane was overlooked or ignored; and today it must be very much as it used to be when Richard Hayes walked or rode along it in the eighteenth century.

Brickhole Lane is the first stage of my round of the Jeskyn's Court Farm which, before the property was sold at the end of the eighteenth century, used to be the Owletts Farm, owned and farmed by the diarist and by his uncle and grandfather before him. At the top of the lane, on the left, is Eleven Acres Orchard, now planted partly with cherries and partly with apples. In the diarist's day it was an arable field. For most of its length, the lane is sunk between high banks. One theory why most steep lanes in this part of the country have high banks is that their surfaces were worn down by the hooves of the generations of sheep and cattle that had been driven up and down them. Another theory is that it was the skid-pans on the back wheels of the lumbering farm wagons that did the damage. Another puts it down to the operations of a wooden implement shaped like a snow-plough which, in the eighteenth century, used to be dragged up and down the roads in the spring in order to smoothe, or "peck out", the winter ruts.

On the right of the lane, the bank is a tangle of elders and blackberries, with an occasional stool of ash, hazel, chestnut and willow. A few of these stumps are tall and old and Rack-hamesque, and look as if they may once have been boundary marks, though what boundary they can ever have marked I do not know, for the arable fields on either side of the lane have always, since the middle of the seventeenth century, been in the possession of a single owner.

On the other side of the lane, after the end of the orchard, there is a thin strip of coppice. This starts by running along the top of the left-hand bank, and then it thickens, and spills down over the bank itself. These strips of coppice, or "shaws", are a typical feature of the landscape of this part of Kent. They were planted partly to serve as wind-breaks, and partly in order to put awkwardly placed bits of land to an economic use. Coppice used to be planted with the same care as conifers are planted today. The rule for a big area of coppice woodland was 1,000 to 1,100 "stools" to the acre. Coppice woodland was, and is, cut down to the stools at eleven or twelve years' intervals, and provides hop-poles, stakes for spile fencing and for hurdles, peasticks, and bavins, which are huge faggots of "tops." Coppice woods are still quite profitable, although the demand for hop-poles has fallen off now that so many hop-gardens are permanently poled and wired; and bakers and lime-burners no longer use bavins to fire their ovens.

The long ridge of continuous woodland at the bottom of the lane comprises Ashenbank on the right, Well Shaw straight ahead, and Chamber's Hill Wood on the left. Ashenbank is a rough, rather ill-organized kind of a wood, a mixture of giant Spanish chestnuts, hornbeams (which grow particularly well in this part of Kent), ashes, oaks, wild cherries and hawthorns. Well Shaw is old, well-established coppice with, at its bottom edge, one or two big elm trees. It gets its name from a chalk

180

well, or dene hole, situated just behind one of the elms. Before
the days of artificial fertilizers, chalk was extracted from these
wells or holes, and was regularly spread on the arable fields.
Some antiquarians still insist that dene holes were storage pits
for grain. I am sure they are wrong. Chamber's Hill Wood
is also coppice, but it has some stands of Scots firs in it, and
quite a lot of silver birches, beeches and larch trees.

A short way down the lane, on the right, there is a badger's
sett in the bank. Every so often the badgers have a spring clean-
ing, and shovel out masses of earth. Half-way down on the left,
at the edge of the lane, there is a hole or pit from which brick
earth used to be dug. Nowadays it is usually full of water in the
wintertime, and "combine" straw is burnt in it in the autumn.
Wherever cherries grow well, the earth is also supposed to be
good for making bricks. I suspect that the earth for the bricks
that were used in the building of my own house came from
this pit. An entry in Richard Hayes's Diary runs:

> 10th February 1771: Carried hurdle gates from Chamber-
> layne's Hill Wood . . . for to fence off ye brick earth my
> Brother's men are digg^g. in order for building him a house
> to live in near the Street.

One of the satisfactory things about taking the same walk or,
in my own case, taking the same route in an electric tricycle,
week after week all through the year is an awareness of the
changing scene and of the changing seasons.

Given a reasonable early spring, the cherry blossom in Eleven
Acres Orchard at the top of Brickhole Lane ought to be full out
by the end of the second week in April; and from this time on
the lane's main attraction is the view it affords of the wooded
ridge that lies ahead. From the beginning of spring until the end
of the autumn, and even right through the winter, colours in
the woods are always changing.

I know now what to look for. For instance—the white patch

of a wild cherry tree in blossom in Ashenbank. It looks all the whiter because it is sandwiched between two starkly bare Spanish chestnuts. The beeches in Chamber's Hill Wood. Even by the beginning of May some of them still look like purple besom brooms, while others are almost full out. The larches that show the brightest green of all. And the elm scrub at the edge of Well Shaw that is covered with a pointillist mist of tiny leaves, while the massed brown leaf buds on the branches of the elms themselves look like clusters of swarming bees.

In high summer, the most dramatic effects are provided by shadows. In the coppice near the bottom of the slope there is a single big ash tree. It overhangs the lane which, on a hot summer's afternoon, can, at this point, turn into a pitch black tunnel, with only lozenges of light filtering through. In the woods themselves there are caverns of black shadows under the rounded tops of the tallest trees. If there is a breeze, the leaves on these topmost branches get turned over, and provide flashes of silver against a background of dark spinachy green. On a summer's evening, one-half of the wheat field that runs up to Ashenbank is a sea of bright yellow light, while the other half is in deep shadow from the tall trees at the edge of the wood.

In the autumn interest switches back to changing colours, and then to the unevenly spaced-out way in which the different trees shed their leaves. Autumn colours should be at their best on or around 28 October. I always look out for one particular maple that grows at the edge of Ashenbank. In Canada, in the autumn, the maple trees turn a flaming red—I once saw mile after mile of them as we sailed down the Gulf of St Lawrence. The Ashenbank maple, seen across a stretch of new, chocolate-brown plough, glitters and glows in the sun like some satisfyingly well-rounded object made of burnished gold. Ashes and apples, I always think, behave oddly. Ashes are lazy brutes. They are almost the last trees to come into leaf, and one of the first to shed their leaves. And their leaves are still green when they fall. Apple leaves remain green and on the trees for a surprisingly long time. Not long ago I noticed a coloured photograph in the *New Yorker*, advertising someone's brandy. Two sportsmen were depicted, standing for some reason in an apple orchard. Also in the picture were a couple of twelve-bore guns, two retrievers, a brace of pheasants lying on the grass, and a bottle of brandy and two glasses disposed on a convenient tree stump. The apple trees were covered with green leaves— and I thought for a moment that the advertisers had been guilty of a frightful howler. Pheasant shooting and apple trees in green leaf hardly seemed to go together. Then I remembered, from the behaviour of the trees in Eleven Acres Orchard, that they quite well could. In the woods themselves I am always surprised how long it takes before all the leaves come off. There are plenty left on the coppice until well after Christmas.

In the winter, according to what kind of a day it is, the woods are either a hard-looking purplish brown, or a misty blue. In either case the dark Scots firs in Chamber's Hill Wood show up very distinctly, and so do the stems of the silver birches. There are some old, long-dead trees in Ashenbank, and their trunks look like silvery-white polished bones. In early April, catkins appear on the hazel coppice, the birds begin singing, and the whole familiar cycle starts all over again.

In the lane itself, the changes are rung against a background of green—provided by the grass on the banks and in the middle of the roadway, the leaves on the coppice, and all the greenstuff, like nettles and dog's-mercury, that grows along any lane anywhere. The first contrasting colour is yellow— celandines and dandelions. After that, for quite a long time, there is symphony in green and white, with a whole succession of white flowers—dead-nettle, cow-parsley, stars of Bethlehem, wood anemones, blackthorn blossom, may, and elder flowers. As a rule I hate elder, and its low corrupting smell; but I have to admit every year that the great creamy white plates of the elder flowers are really rather handsome. There are quite a lot of

183

bluebells in the coppice, but they do not contrive to make much of an impression. After the elder has stopped flowering, the lane reverts to all-green again, the greens getting darker and darker.

Brickhole Lane is one of the reasons why, as I hope, I shall not miss publishing too much, and why, as I confidently expect, I shall be happy and contented living all the time in the country. The round of the farm to which the lane is a prelude is another reason. There are two hop-gardens sheltering under the lea of Well Shaw and Chamber's Hill Wood. One of them, Lower Scotland Field, was a hop-garden, or "ground" as he would have called it, in Richard Hayes's time. I have no intention of boring anyone by reciting the various processes of hop-growing and hop-cultivating that go on right through the year. But these gardens, and the things that happen in them, are a perpetual interest to me. And there are any number of other things that I see from my chair which suggest questions to which I try from time to time to find the answers. How long, for instance, have these familiar woods been in existence? If they are not surviving fragments of an aboriginal forest, who planted them, and why? And how did they get their sometimes very odd names? How, when and why did the roads and lanes in the parish first come into existence? Why do some of them run straight, while others twist about all over the place? There is one lane in this village that, until it was straightened some years ago, suddenly and for no apparent reason ran round three sides of a square. I discovered that the square had once been occupied by a manor house which had been long demolished. And why are the fields the shapes and sizes they are? Is the present-day pattern old, fairly old, or comparatively recent?

Solving these and similar conundrums would keep a much more effective village historian than I shall ever be busy for a long lifetime. And they represent much less than half the battle.

In any village, successive generations of great and small

184

landowners, parsons, farmers, smallholders, tradesmen, craftsmen and farmworkers have lived, down the years, in a succession of houses, have organized their lives and have worked and
worshipped and enjoyed themselves in a succession of different
ways, and have left their records, even if they consist only in a
few scattered entries in the church register. In any village there
are landmarks which are as much a part of the landscape as the
fields, woods and roads. The village church, for instance; the
village street with its houses, pubs and shops; a great house,
perhaps, in its surrounding park; outlying farms; a mill. As
time has passed, these landmarks will have changed—some of
them radically. A few will have disappeared altogether. New
landmarks will have made their appearance.

How people live their lives today, and how they lived them in
comparatively recent times—say fifty, one hundred, or two
hundred years ago—should, in my view, be just as much the
concern of the village historian as the scattered sarsen stones
which may once have formed part of a pre-Bronze Age megalith,
or the remains of a Roman villa. It used to infuriate me at school
when, having reached the accession of Queen Victoria in whatever text-book of English history we used, we were made to
turn back and start all over again with the Norman Conquest.
I have little patience with local historians who, in giving a
detailed account of a parish church, dismiss its Victorian restoration in a few scornful words. I am passionately interested in
when the railway station that serves my own village was built,
and when it was first opened to traffic; in when the present-day
cowled oast-houses replaced the older square-shaped oasts; and
in when the public houses changed their names, and why.

I do not mean to suggest for a moment that the village
historian should ignore the most important, and probably the
most interesting, landmarks in his parish—simply because they
may already be pretty well documented. In my time I have
written a guide-book to Cobham Hall; and I have compiled
notes on Cobham Church and on the College of St Mary's.

Each of these three notable, indeed outstanding, buildings had already been written about by scores of eighteenth- and nineteenth-century antiquarians. My own efforts merely confirmed an impression that no one has yet begun to find out the half of what there is to be found out about them.

Trying to write the guide to the Hall—I was asked by Lord Darnley to produce a small booklet when he decided to open the house and its grounds to the public—fulfilled my old Oxford ambition to be let loose in the muniment room of a stately home. Experience often falls short of expectation. I had pictured myself picking my leisurely way through well-arranged papers in a cosy room at the top of the house; and breaking off from my note-taking each afternoon to drink a cup of tea with the house's noble owner in the shade of a giant cedar tree on a well-shaved lawn. It had always, in my dreams, been high summer. I tackled the Cobham Hall records one winter when Lord Darnley and his family were in the South of France, and when the house was deserted and unheated. Week-end after week-end I sat huddled in my thickest greatcoat in the small library in the south wing. It might have been pretty cold out of doors when I set out. I knew it would be ten degrees colder when I got inside the Hall.

Nor were the muniments in apple-pie order. The 7th Earl of Darnley, whose short reign ended in 1900, had been, to say the least of it, a bit eccentric. His temper, apparently, was short; and one of the ways in which he had vented it had been to make huge bonfires of documents and letters in the forecourt. These he would ignite and then, according to unreliable reports, he would dance angrily round the resulting blaze. Goodness knows what treasures may have perished in these holocausts. His successor's wife, the grandmother of the present earl, was an Australian lady of great charm and beauty, who set herself the task of salvaging and collecting up such records as had survived. But the methods she employed would hardly have commended themselves to a trained archivist. She bundled up papers, deeds and documents, disregarding dates, subjects and provenance,

186

and stuffed them into a series of shoe-boxes. To have possessed so many boxes she must, in her day, have bought a prodigious number of pairs of shoes. Or perhaps she bought them by the gross from a box manufacturer. I never had any idea of what I might come on next. Letters written to the 3rd Earl in 1770 and 1771 about the alterations and additions to the house that were then in full swing rubbed shoulders with Christmas cards from King George V and Queen Mary and programmes of village concerts held between 1900 and 1914. The brief prepared for Counsel in the matter of the 4th Earl's claim to the Dukedom of Lenox (it never came to anything) shared a box with his grandson's vitriolic exchange of letters with his neighbour, the Marquess of Abergavenny, who, at a West Kent Hunt dinner, had had the temerity to suggest that the owner of Cobham Hall was a vulpicide. By the time I had finished with them the Cobham Hall papers were probably in an even worse mess than they had been in before. Now, I am pleased to say, they have been properly arranged and catalogued.

My next task, when I can get round to it, will be to try to write an account of the College of St Mary's—the forerunner of the present-day almshouses which lie immediately to the south of the church. I want to find out, if I can, what life was really like in a small college of chantry priests in the fifteenth century. Lately, I have been concentrating on how life was lived by the Cobham villagers in the nineteenth century; and in this connection I have had two strokes of luck.

I had often wondered how, before the National Insurance Act came into operation and after the overseers of the poor had disappeared, farm labourers and other villagers had fared when they were off work through sickness or injury. Many of them still had no regular employers. I found the answer, so far as Cobham was concerned, in "The United Services Benefit Society." A copy of the Articles of Agreement of this Society turned up when a very old lady in the village died. It had been started in the year 1829 with the following stated purpose: "As

187

brotherly love and charitable friendship are duties in which mankind should strictly join, the Members of this Society most cheerfully agree to support each other under such calamities which Almighty God may please to afflict us with. . . ." To be eligible for membership, a man had to live within six miles of the Darnley Arms public house in Cobham Street; there were quarterly meetings when each member paid in the sum of 5s., "out of which 4d. shall be spent on beer, and the remainder to go to the box"; and if a paid-up member was prevented "by sickness or lameness" from following his occupation, he "went on the club" and received 10s. a week. Each Whit-Monday the Society held its annual feast. On these occasions 2s. was taken from the box for each member, and each member paid in a similar sum. All the fines and forfeits collected during the preceding twelve months—and the Articles bristled with financial penalties for every conceivable misdemeanour, misbehaviour, and evasion of duties and responsibilities—were spent on this beano, which began with compulsory attendance at a church service, and finished up with a procession down the village street led by a brass band. The Articles were revised in 1865, and again in 1880. This self-help version of the Welfare State flourished, and managed triumphantly to remain solvent to the end.

My second stroke of luck was someone else's discovery, in a mass of rubbish destined for the dustman, of a series of spirited caricatures of some of the regular customers of the Darnley Arms in the years 1890 and 1894. There they all were—the postman, the potman, a soldier on leave, the Jeskyn's farm hop-dryer, and several of the old gentlemen from the college—depicted in their everyday clothes and with their pipes and their mugs of beer. And although, in the best traditions of "Ape" and "Spy", only nicknames were scrawled under each sketch, dashed off either on a sheet of cardboard or on the back of a card advertising a local brand of mineral water, there was no question about the identity of the sitters. They were easily recognized by elderly inhabitants of the village, who declared that the likeness, in each case, was a "speaking" one. I discovered that the artist had been one Cecil Schott, who was Fanny Cornforth's stepson. Schott had been commissioned to copy, or to restore, some of the old master paintings in the picture gallery at Cobham Hall. He had lodged in the village, had gone to the Darnley Arms each evening, and had been happy to paint anyone's portrait for the price of a pint of beer.

No village ought to remain static; and while some developments are a bit hard to swallow, the impact of drastic changes on a small, closely knit and long-established community are interesting to watch. Cobham has recently experienced two "revolutions"—one universally welcomed, the other pretty generally deplored.

Cobham Hall, purchased by the Minister of Works in order to save a splendid but over-large and unwieldy mansion from decay and eventual demolition, has opened as a brand new girls' public school. Watching the restoration of a house that I feared was irretrievably doomed gave me enormous pleasure—akin to witnessing the miraculous recovery of an old friend who had supposedly been stricken with an incurable illness. And I like to think of generations of schoolgirls cheerfully dispelling the gloom that lately haunted the deserted south terrace when I used to trundle along it in my chair on a still, misty November afternoon. Then the great empty house, its derelict gardens, and its park seemed to be held in a vice of uncanny silence and immobility.

The second innovation has been the abrupt arrival in our midst of fifty gipsy caravans. The immediate reaction was one of consternation. Our primary school, it was argued, would be swamped. It was unfair suddenly to increase the village's population by some three hundred people whose way of life was different from the way of life of the villagers. These gipsies could not be genuine travelling people—because the last thing that they apparently wanted to do was to travel. We were told

189

by their champion that we must take these newcomers to our hearts, integrate them into the life of the village, and help them to become solid citizens. We were reminded that Cobham had strong Dickensian associations, and that Dickens would have deplored our Scrooge-like attitude. It occurred to me to wonder what Charles Dickens would in fact have said if a gipsy encampment had been established in the near neighbourhood of Gad's Hill Place. It will be interesting to see what happens. In a novel, a golden-haired village child would be stolen by these mysterious caravan-dwellers, and their camp would be attacked and burnt by infuriated villagers. In real life, things generally work out rather differently; and by the end of two years—the proposed duration of this experiment—we may possibly have grown quite fond of our gipsies. For all I know, their offspring may decide to conduct a survey of the parish, teaching me in the process a lot of things that I have never discovered for myself.

*   *   *

Lightweight anecdotes? Parish pump gossip? Small beer? I know. And that goes, too, I am afraid, for all the other chapters in this book. There have been, up to the present, no important achievements in my life on which I can look back with pride. I have made no lasting or significant contributions to historical research, to literature, or to the art and practice of publishing. In a material sense, save for a maddening physical disability, I have been undeservedly lucky. Circumstances have allowed me, within reason, to do more or less what I have wanted to do—or what, at any given time, I thought that I wanted to do. I have led a very quiet, a very happy and, I hope, a comparatively harmless life.

I lately considered the whole matter as objectively as I could; and I decided that there was one thing that might be said in mitigation of an ill-organized and largely trivial career. I have very seldom embarked on any enterprise, however pointless, without bringing it to some sort of conclusion, however unsuccessful.